WEIRD WAR 2

WEIRD WAR 2

Richard Denham
With an introduction by
M J Trow

This edition published 2016 worldwide by T Squared Books.
www.tsquaredbooks.co.uk

Cover art by M. J. Trow

A CIP catalogue record for this book is available from the British Library

ISBN: 978-0-9954521-6-9 (paperback)

T SQUARED BOOKS

‘The war, though we dislike it quite a bit,
Is sometimes laughable, you must admit.’

A.P. Herbert *Badogliovski*
Sunday Graphic 1945

FOREWORD

Weird; *out of the ordinary, strange, unusual ... odd, bizarre, incomprehensible.*

New Shorter Oxford English Dictionary

Welcome to the wonderfully weird World War Two.

There is a rose-tinted sentimentality today that the '40s were some utopian golden age and we have been sliding downhill ever since. My grandparents certainly believed this. As I grew up and developed an interest in the Second World War, I realised that it wasn't quite like that. It was heroic and courageous; but it was also confusing; devastating; nightmarish and bizarre, words that we can't equate with the 'good old days.'

Fond memories of ration books and making-do-and-mending, are offset by appalling brutality and loss of life. For every GI in a dance hall there was a concentration camp prisoner; for every daring commando there was a starving Soviet; for every fanatical SS officer there was a conscript who really had no choice. This book tries to touch on it all.

I have decided not to add sources and citations because this is essentially a whistle-stop recap of tales. There is still so much from the Second World War that experts do not agree on and many subjects remain disputed and controversial.

Many of the facts you are about to read are by no means certain. Some of the facts aren't necessarily what actually happened, but what has been reported to have happened and wars always involve rumour; it is part of the psychology of conflict. I have deliberately tried to keep the writing style as light-hearted and non-confrontational as the horrors of war allow, and I would like to apologise in advance if I have written anything that offends.

My father was a soldier in the British Army and I enjoyed the stories he would tell me as a child. Though he recalled his military career fondly, he forbade me from ever joining up. One quote will always stick with me, 'Life's too short; thank God I never have to go through any of that bollocks ever again.' I like to think that is a sentiment shared by all veterans and survivors of the countless conflicts throughout the world ever since the Second World War.

The world truly was on the brink of destruction, but by some miracle we pulled through. With a conflict that will soon pass from living memory, we owe it to the survivors to know what they suffered. We don't have to judge; we just have to know. Forgiven, but not forgotten.

I would like to take this opportunity to thank M J Trow for his excellent introduction. Whether you know a lot or a little about the Second World War, I do encourage you to read it; you will find his masterly summing up a useful starting point before you begin.

I was trying, as this book came together, to find a kind of rule of thumb of how bizarre something was, from weird to weirder to weirdest and you will find from one to three exclamation marks above the title on each page.

Welcome to Weird War Two…

Richard Denham
2016

INTRODUCTION

The Second World War 1939-45

The Causes

The older generation still call it 'Hitler's War' but monumental events that lead to the deaths of millions cannot be placed at any one man's door. To understand how war came about in September 1939 we have to go back to the Treaty of Versailles that ended the First World War.

The victors at Versailles – Britain, France, Italy and the United States – decided that Germany had caused the First World War (which they hadn't) and that Germany must pay. To that end, territory which once belonged to Germany was taken away, German armed forces were cut to almost non-existence and the country was saddled with a massive reparations bill of £3.5 billion (at least $46 billion today) and it couldn't possibly pay.

The weak democratic Weimar government struggled on for ten years, but the financial disaster of October 1929 – the Wall Street crash – plunged Germany particularly deeply into recession and that gave a new impetus to Adolf Hitler's National Socialist party, which, until then, had been regarded as something of a lunatic fringe. In a series of underhand political manoeuvres, Hitler became Chancellor of Germany in 1933 and set up a state he promised would last a thousand years – the Third Reich. In fact, it lasted just twelve and a half years and the steps that led to the Second World War also led to Germany's second defeat in thirty years.

The Steps to War 1933-39

1933 Hitler becomes Chancellor of a bitter and angry Germany.

1934 On the death of President Hindenberg, Hitler becomes President, giving himself the title *Fuhrer* (leader).
All members of the German army (Wehrmacht), air force (Luftwaffe) and navy (Kriegsmarine) swear a personal oath of allegiance to Hitler.

1935 In an Anglo-German naval agreement, Germany is allowed to build warships again.
Saarland (Germany's smallest federal state) is returned to Germany after a referendum, having been removed from its control as part of the Treaty of Versailles.

1936 Hitler invades the demilitarized Rhineland, devoid of troops since Versailles, claiming that he has that right. Britain and France complain but do nothing.
Civil war breaks out in Spain and Hitler supplies General Francisco Franco's Fascists with aircraft, experts and cash. The Luftwaffe's Condor Legion bombs Guernica, giving the world the first taste of Blitzkrieg (Lightning War).
The Rome-Berlin Axis (the Pact of Steel) is signed between Hitler and Benito Mussolini, the Fascist duce (leader) of Italy, but not ratified until three years later.
Germany and Japan sign the Anti-Comintern Pact against the left wing countries of the Communist International, spearheaded by Russia (the Union of Socialist Soviet Republics).

1938 The *Anschluss* with Austria. On the face of it, a peaceful union, it is actually a Nazi coup.
Hitler claims the Sudetenland, part of the new state of Czechoslovakia, as German because of the large number of Germans living there. He needs *lebensraum* (living space) for his rapidly growing country.
At the Munich Conference in September, Hitler promises Neville Chamberlain, the British Prime Minister and Edouard Daladier, his French counterpart, that he has no further ambitions in Europe.

1939 Ignoring Munich, Hitler invades Prague and Memel in March.
Anxious to expand to the east and to regain East Prussia, Hitler signs a non-aggression pact with Josef Stalin, the Russian leader.

Two days later, Britain signs an agreement with Poland that is clearly Hitler's short-term target. On a pretext, on 1 September, Hitler launches *Fall Weiss* (Case White) and invades Poland.

On 3 September, with Hitler ignoring Chamberlain's ultimatum to withdraw his troops, Britain declares war on Nazi Germany. So does France.

The Second World War has begun.

The Phoney War 1939-40

The French called it the Funny War (Drôle de Guerre); to the Germans it was Sitzkrieg (the Armchair War). The British coined the word 'phoney' from an article by an American journalist based in London. In the west, nothing happened. The east was a different story, however. Poland fell in the September War, crushed between Hitler's Germany and Stalin's Russia and the execution squads of the einsatzgruppen went to work rounding up and shooting Jews – another step towards the Holocaust.

There was action at sea too. Two British aircraft carriers, the newest and most expensive ships afloat, had been sunk by October, and there were air raids on British naval bases in Scotland. The Kriegsmarine's pocket battleship, the *Admiral Graf Spee* was scuttled by her crew in the River Plate on 17 December. In terms of military capability, the Royal Navy had the edge, but the Luftwaffe, whose aircraft had been built secretly for years, were far ahead of the Royal Air Force, thanks to years of appeasement under Prime Ministers Baldwin and Chamberlain. In November, the USSR invaded Finland. This was the Winter War, in which the Finns, with their local knowledge, proved more than a match for the Red Army.

With spectacular mistiming, Neville Chamberlain told that House of Commons that, in delaying an all-out attack in the west, Hitler had 'missed the bus'. Five days later, the Germans invaded Norway.

Collapse of the West 1940

It was the British who had misread the bus timetable! Norway was crucial to both sides, because of its strategic position overlooking the North Atlantic and its production of heavy water. The Germans moved first and despite a half-hearted British involvement, overran the country and set up a puppet government under Vidkun Quisling, whose name became synonymous with traitor (in fact, he had never made any secret of his Nazi sympathies). Denmark, hopelessly feeble against the power of the Reich, surrendered after only one day and the threat to flatten Copenhagen. Of the 16,000 troops in the Danish army, only thirteen were killed.

Failure in Norway led to a no-confidence vote in the Commons and Chamberlain was forced to resign. His replacement, on 10 May, was the First Lord of the Admiralty, Winston Churchill. He had been warning of the Nazi threat for years and this was to be his finest hour.

Churchill's first day at Number Ten was the start of *Fall Gelb* (Case Yellow), the simultaneous invasion of Holland, Belgium and France. On paper, the Allied and Axis armies were exactly matched but no one was prepared for the speed of the German advance under blitzkrieg. Aerial attacks, using a mixture of bombers (*Heinkels* and *Dorniers*) and fighters (*Messerschmitts* and *Stukas*) were followed by pincer movements on the ground spearheaded by the *panzers*, the tanks that had replaced horsed cavalry. The Allies had no leaders of the calibre of Heinz Guderian, Erwin Rommel and Gerd von Rundstedt and despite valiant defence, Holland surrendered in five days.

A British expeditionary force was rushed to France (exactly as in 1914) but was driven back to the coast at Dunkirk. The 'miracle' that happened there was the result of private boats – 'the little ships of England' – that crossed the Channel and carried back as many men as they could. It was all part of Churchill's genius that he turned what was actually an embarrassing defeat into a victory and the 'Dunkirk spirit' is still occasionally heard of today. Belgium surrendered at the end of May and France soon after. The armistice was signed in the same railway carriage at Compiegne where the Germans had surrendered in 1918 and an ecstatic Hitler went sightseeing in Paris. Versailles was avenged.

The People's War 1940-41

The summer of 1940 has become the 'Spitfire Summer'. Hitler's invasion of Britain – Operation Sealion – was heralded by the blitzkrieg tactic of knocking out the RAF first. All over the south east of the country, dogfights were fought daily in what became known as the Battle of Britain, but the RAF – 'the few' as Churchill called them – held out and Herman Goering, head of the

Luftwaffe, was forced to change tack and bomb civilian cities instead.

'The Blitz', beginning in earnest on 30 August, is a prime example of Britain's 'finest hour'. Guernica came to London, Coventry, Plymouth and Hull. Industrial, war production areas were the target but the bombing technology of 1940 was not that precise and homes, schools, hospitals and *people* were all caught up in it. A paranoid government, convinced that there was a Fifth Column of spies operating in the country, gave draconian powers to the police, the armed forces and an army of 'little Hitlers' in and out of uniform, to curb civil liberties. Much of this has never gone away. Bombing raids, the blackout, spivs selling rationed goods illegally on the black market, all this became part of a legend. By May 1941, 40,000 British civilians had been killed, another 46,000 badly injured. Over a million homes were shattered. But the world learned a lesson that still has to be driven home – mass bombing does not lead to collapse; it just increases resistance.

The Wider War 1941-42

Countries overrun by the Germans coped as best they could. Most people kept their heads down and did as they were told. Some collaborated openly – Quisling in Norway, Marshal Petain in Vichy France. Others resisted, either passively or actively, like the Maquis in France, sabotaging German occupation and staying in touch by radio with Britain, now 'fortress Britain', standing alone.

With dreams of recreating another Roman Empire, Mussolini sent his troops into North Africa in June 1940. Egypt had been in British hands since the nineteenth century and General Archibald Wavell stopped the Italians at Sidi Birrani in December. It was depressing proof to Hitler that his Italian allies weren't worth the candle and he sent in Erwin Rommel and his Afrika Korps to bail them out. Wavell was beaten back.

The extraordinarily tortuous politics of the Balkans re-emerged, resulting in a German attack on the new state of Yugoslavia (today's Croatia) and the invasion of Greece. The British attempt to police the Mediterranean (they had Gibraltar at the western end, Malta in the centre and Cyprus in the east) met with disaster and Crete fell to the Germans by June 1941.

On the 22nd of that month, Hitler made the biggest mistake of the war by launching Operation Barbarossa, the invasion of the USSR. This had been his plan all along, taking *lebensraum* to a logical conclusion and Josef Stalin seemed blissfully unaware. The long drawn out Eastern Front saw the deaths of millions. To the Russians, it was the Patriotic War, defending their own territory against a treacherous enemy. Stalin was quite prepared to sacrifice as many millions as it took. For their part, the Germans had underestimated both the tenacity of the enemy and the severity of the Russian winter. Petrol froze in the tanks of mechanised transport and blitzkrieg ground to a halt in sieges like Stalingrad.

On 7 December – 'a day that will live in infamy' as President Franklin D Roosevelt said – the Japanese bombed the US naval base at Pearl Harbor in the Hawaiian Islands. America had sat on an isolationist fence throughout the Twenties and Thirties, its population made up of the descendants of both sides who faced each other in 1939. Roosevelt's natural inclination was to join the Allies but there was a powerful German lobby at home and he had promised America's mothers that their boys would not be involved. Instead, the Lend-Lease programme was set up – vital money and equipment lent to Britain (the debt was finally repaid in 1994).

Japanese ambitions in the Pacific (they had been at war with China since 1937) were unrealistic. America's actual military strength in 1941 was feeble, but the wealth of the country and its military capability were awesome. The 'double whammy' of Barbarossa and Pearl Harbor in the same year made it inevitable that Hitler would lose the war.

Initially, the Japanese did well, driving the British out of Singapore in one of the most embarrassing defeats in modern history. The creation of the Burma railway, where thousands of British prisoners of war were worked to death, ranks alongside the Holocaust in terms of inhumanity, although of course the numbers going routinely to the gas chambers of Europe by 1943 have no comparison.

Now that Soviet Russia had joined the Allied camp, there was need to relieve them as far as possible. Convoys of British merchant ships ploughed the icy waters of the North Atlantic to achieve this, at the mercy of the dreaded Kriegsmarine U Boats. A huge propaganda coup was struck when the iconic new battleship the *Bismarck* was sunk by the British in May 1941.

Turning Points 1942-43

We have already seen how important Hitler's decision to invade

Russia was. The attack on Pearl Harbor was another gamble too far. In the Pacific, the Americans fought back at the battle of Midway, in which the Japanese lost four aircraft carriers, 332 aircraft and 3,500 men.

In July, Bernard Montgomery's British Eighth Army stopped Rommel's Afrika Korps at El Alamein, near Alexandria and Operation Torch saw the invasion of Italian-held Morocco, Algeria and Tunisia by the British and Americans.

In the east, the Wehrmacht was losing men daily at an horrific rate and by 31 January 1943, General Friedrich von Paulus was forced to surrender the Sixth Army.

The Invasion of Europe 1942-44

With Rommel's Afrika Korps destroyed and the Italians on the run, an Anglo-American force invaded Sicily and Italy, making for Rome. It was the first assault of Hitler's Europe-wide Reich and one of its first casualties was Mussolini, kicked out by his own government and put under house arrest. Stiffened by the Germans, Italy held on for months, fighting battles at Anzio and Monte Cassino, but in the end, they surrendered and were effectively out of the war by the end of 1943.

In the summer of that year, the Red Army under General Georgy Zhukov began to push the exhausted Wehrmacht back to the German border they had crossed with such high hopes during Barbarossa two years earlier. Zhukov's ultimate destination was Berlin.

For the RAF it was payback time. With the USAAF flying out from British bases, Air Chief Marshal Arthur 'Bomber' Harris unleashed raids on German cities. Dresden was hit by a firestorm unparalleled in history and today Harris is regarded by many as a war criminal. In fact, he was just doing his job and no one at the time had a problem with that.

All of this was crowned on 6 June 1944 by Operation Overlord, the biggest amphibious assault in history. 27,000 airborne troops had landed in Normandy the previous night to take vital bridgeheads and road crossings before the 'ducks' ran up the beaches codenamed Omaha, Utah, Sword, Gold and Juno. The Germans were caught napping. Only at 'bloody Omaha' was there serious resistance; Rommel was on leave in Germany at the time and Hitler dithered. The next weeks after D Day (D for Deliverance) saw the Allies driving the Wehrmacht across France, liberating towns and villages as they went.

The Race for Berlin 1944-45

By the end of September 1944, twenty-five of thirty-seven German divisions of Army Group Centre had been destroyed by the Red Army. Berlin was panicking – the Cossacks were on the German border and the Communist threat had never loomed so starkly. By the end of the year, the Germans had pulled out of the Balkans, consolidating and regrouping to defend their homeland.

1944 saw a sting in the tail with the return of the Blitz over Britain. Hitler's rocket scientists, working on jet and unmanned aircraft technology, came out with the V1 and V2 missiles – 'doodlebugs' – that rained down on British cities as conventional bombs had three years earlier.

Advancing steadily from the west, the Allies, under the command of General Dwight Eisenhower, drove all before them. There were disagreements as to how exactly this should be done and hotheads like Montgomery and George Patton constantly clashed. Operation Market Garden, an airborne attempt to capture the bridges at Arnhem, was a disaster however with a loss of life that was all the harder to take because the end of the war was now surely in sight. In a last ditch gamble, the Germans attacked in the Ardennes forest – the battle of the Bulge. Probably only a lack of equipment meant that it failed.

At the beginning of 1945, Hitler became increasingly delusional. The Allies crossed the Rhine in February and March as the Russians swept through eastern Germany to take territory they would refuse to give up for forty years. In the event, it was the Red Army that got to Berlin first, fighting street by street for the enemy capital. The names of some of them are still there, scratched into the plaster of the Reichstag, Berlin's parliament building. In an appalling act which the Russians still deny, thousands of German women and girls were raped by Soviet troops.

Gotterdammerung 1945

Hitler was hiding in his bunker under Berlin while the fighting raged overhead. On 29 April he married his mistress Eva Braun and they committed suicide, either by poison or gunshot (exact details are unclear) and their bodies were doused in petrol and burned. Admiral Karl Doenitz was Hitler's successor, all other leading Nazis now on the run and he negotiated the Reich's surrender over the next few days. 8 May was officially designated VE (Victory in Europe) Day and there were street parties all over Britain and the newly-liberated countries of the west.

In the far east, General William Slim's 14th Army drove the Japanese out of Burma and the Americans captured island after island in the South Pacific ('island hopping', it was called). Iwo Jima and Okinawa became enshrined in American folklore as a result but it was felt that everyone was too exhausted to go on; and to the Japanese, surrender was unthinkable. With that in mind, the new president, Harry S Truman, authorised the first use of the newly-created atomic bomb. 'Little Boy' and 'Fat Boy' flattened the cities of Hiroshima and Nagasaki, bringing nuclear terror to the world with which we all still live. In seventeen seconds at Hiroshima, 80,000 people were dead with a further 70,000 badly injured. VJ Day (Victory in Japan) was officially 15 August.

What next?

As the Allies liberated German-held Europe, the reality of the Holocaust came to light. Six million people, Jews, homosexuals, gypsies and political dissidents had been exterminated in death camps like Auschwitz, Dachau and Treblinka. The Nazi high command scattered but most of them were captured and faced trial for war crimes at Nuremberg, the scene of the pre-war Nazi rallies, in 1946. Sixteen of the twenty-one were hanged by the British executioner Albert Pierrepoint.

Various high level Allied conferences over the last two years of the war set out the post-war world. Soviet Russia refused to hand back captured German territories and used the war as an opportunity to extend the limits of the Soviet bloc to include large sections of eastern Europe that had never been either Communist or Russian. Germany itself was divided between the Allies, east and west Berlin suffering the same fate. Winston Churchill, ousted in a post-war election, prophesied that an 'iron curtain' would come down across Europe and so it proved, leading to the Cold War and espionage fictions without number.

A devastated world struggled to come to terms with what had happened, rebuilding, reshaping and trying to forget the past. But some things – the Holocaust, the blanket bombing, the Burma railway, the A bomb – are unforgettable. We will always have them with us.

!
Ahnenpass

Central to the ideology of the Third Reich was the concept of race. Only those who could claim pure Aryan blood going back four generations were allowed to hold professional posts in government, the armed forces, teaching and the law.

Parenting in the Nazi mindset was everything; to be a pure German was essential to have much chance of having a successful life. As well as 'pure' Aryans and 'full' Jews, there were also those with three, two or just one Jewish grandparent and various government officials spent years defining various categories. Even a German who was just one quarter Jewish was considered to be a '*Mischling* (mixed-blood) of the second degree'. The *Ahnenpass* (ancestor passport) was another of the countless forms and papers to come out of the Reich, a state obsessed with paperwork. It wasn't an official government document, but a way for Germans to prove their Aryan parentage by tracing and documenting their family tree. Eventually it would be needed to go to school or get married. The work of tracing family trees was difficult and arduous (long before the internet!), relying on people tracking down their own family trees via church and civil records. Unsurprisingly, the services of genealogists rocketed during the Reich.

Such an arbitrary system could be turned on its head, although many women were successful in court in convincing the judge that any offspring with Jewish fathers were the results of adultery with Aryans. Bribery and corruption was also rife in the justice system with back-handers ensuring people weren't classified as mixed-blood. Sometimes on the whim of the leadership, Jewish ancestry would be 'forgiven' and people would be given Aryan blood certificates. A classic example was Erhard Milch, a *Wehrmacht* field marshal with a Jewish father. It is possible that up to 160,000 *mischlinge* fought for Hitler during the war. The *Ahnenpass* was available in all good book stores and cost 0.60 Reichsmarks

!
'And All That Jazz!'

Nazi ideology frowned on much that was acceptable elsewhere and Jazz, which was spreading in popularity around the world as the party grew, came in for special criticism. It was popular in Germany at the time but was classified by the Nazis as 'degenerate negro music seen through the eyes of Jews'. Performances by black musicians were banned in Germany in 1932 and by 1935 they were not allowed to be heard on the radio.

Interestingly, similar doubts were being expressed in America, but there it was more of a generational issue, rather as rock 'n' roll would horrify the Moms and Dads who fought the Second World War. A rebellious group in Germany, 'The Swing Kids', continued to listen to Jazz music in private and opposed the Hitler Youth and League of German Maidens. Over three hundred Swing Kids were arrested in 1941, their punishments ranging from having their hair cropped to being sent to concentration camps.

Despite all this, Josef Goebbels still found a place for Jazz music in his propaganda repertoire. Lead by front man Karl 'Charlie' Schwedler, Charlie and His Orchestra became a surreal part of the propaganda machine in 1940. The band would play Swing and Jazz classics to their listeners in Britain every Wednesday and Saturday at 9pm but with altered lyrics, supposedly with the help of 'Lord Haw-Haw' (William Joyce), boasting of the strength of the Reich and mocking Churchill and the Allied war effort. Their cover of Walter Donaldson's 'You're Driving Me Crazy' contains a bizarre section of Schwedler impersonating Churchill, being driven crazy by the military might of the Nazis and the Jews. The ominously upbeat 'Let's Go Bombing' gives us the cheery point of view of a raid on neutral areas, civilians and churches far from the areas of conflict.

The band was broken up after the war, but treated leniently and most of them continued to have successful musical careers.

!!!

Anti-tank Dogs

Animals and warfare have been linked for centuries. Horses charged into battle and pulled war chariots; pigeons carried messages in the First World War; dogs pulled equipment sledges over frozen battlefields.

For dog lovers, their deployment in the Second World War was perhaps going too far. The idea was particularly popular with the Russians, who carried on using anti-tank dogs until the nineties! As the name suggests, the dogs were strapped with explosives and trained to run under German tanks and use their teeth to release the bomb before running back to safety. The second part of this proved too difficult however, and it was thought more effective for the dogs to be blown up once they reached their target. The training of this involved leaving the dogs' food under tanks, so they instinctively learned to run under any tank to find their supper. Quite how the food was to be put there in the first place is not clear!

Anti-tank dogs did not always (unlike most Nazis) follow orders. In the confusion and noise of battle, having had their explosives primed, the animals would often run back to their handlers, leading to a grisly end for both of them. Of the first thirty dogs deployed on the Eastern Front against the Reich, four blew up under German tanks and six blew up returning to their handlers.

!
The Armistice Carriage

Nothing typifies the contempt that Hitler felt for the French more than his use of the Armistice carriage in 1940. The original train belonged to Marechal Ferdinand Foch and was chosen for the signing of the 1918 armistice because the siding in the quiet forest of Compiegne, thirty-seven miles north of Paris, was remote and discreet. The train was briefly still in use after the First World Warbut then was handed over to the Army Museum in Paris.

Hitler, bitter and humiliated, as were many Germans, by losing the first World War, clearly remembered this. The blitzkrieg against France in 1940 was overwhelming, the Wehrmacht simply bypassing the Maginot Line with its impenetrable line of fortifications by going through Belgium. When France sued for peace against the Reich, Hitler insisted the surrender be offered inside the very train carriage of 1918. He had it removed from the Army Museum and returned to the exact same spot it had been in in November during the first armistice. In fact, he deliberately sat in Foch's seat of 1918 when France officially surrendered to him on 21 June. This was not, said Colonel General von Keitel on the day itself, an act of revenge, but merely to right a wrong.

The carriage was then taken to Germany where it was on display in Berlin until 1943. It remained there until it was destroyed by the SS in Thuringia in 1945.

!!
Atlantis

Heinrich Himmler, as Reichsfuhrer of the SS, was a man fascinated by mysticism and the foundations of 'Aryan' history. Many of the stories of his obsession for the occult that have survived seem rather far-fetched and the archaeology of the Nazis has been fertile ground for conspiracy theorists ever since, even finding its way into the Indiana Jones film franchise starring Harrison Ford.

It is known that many expeditions were conducted by the Nazis under the *Ahnenerbe*, a department set up to find evidence of the Aryan racial theory and history and personally run by Himmler.

Atlantis, mentioned by Plato, Aristotle and various writers of the ancient world, was a highly advanced and sophisticated civilization destroyed, according to legend, in a single day by some unknown catastrophe. Whether Himmler actually believed this or simply wanted to create a mythology for propaganda purposes is a matter of opinion but either way he put great efforts into the pursuit of it. The *Ahnenerbe* thought that Atlantis could have been a sunken island somewhere between Britain and Portugal – Plato refers to the Pillars of Hercules, i.e. the Straits of Gibraltar – and that those who survived made it to Tibet over 5,000 miles away. A team of scientists and archaeologists travelled there where they used their pseudo-science to study the faces and head-shapes of the locals and decided they were in fact descended from the Atlanteans. However, in the Nazi view of racial purity, the bloodline had been poisoned by interbreeding with the Tibetans.

One theory that interested Himmler in the legend of the lost civilization of Atlantis was the idea the survivors were Aryans, thereby explaining why there was no archaeological evidence of an ancient Aryan culture.

!!
Balloon Bombs

One of the more bizarre facts of history is that war gives a stimulus to technology and more money has been spent on arms manufacture than anything to do with peace. Leonardo da Vinci is today remembered as a genius, a 'universal man' renowned as a painter, sculptor and theoretical physicist; but he made his money designing weapons for various Italian noblemen.

No less ingenious were the Japanese in the Second World War. Harnessing the power of jet streams that blew east across the Pacific Ocean, they came up with the idea of balloon bombs. The idea was relatively simple; explosives attached to paper balloons. These bombs would then float silently to the USA and cause untold damage, the brilliance of the weapon lying in the fact that there was no way to stop it until it detonated.

First created in 1944, the balloons were launched from Japan, taking approximately 30 to 60 hours to reach their destination. The first was launched on 3 November. Figures vary wildly but it is estimated that between 1,000 and 9,000 balloon bombs were created and sent to the west coast of America. Only 284 were discovered according to American reports.

The US government were quick to hide these balloon bombs from the general public, and they appeared to be ineffective, but there was one tragedy. On 5 May 1945, a group of five children and a pregnant woman having a picnic in Bly, Oregon, came across one of the balloons. With no reason to suspect it was a bomb, they accidentally detonated it, becoming part of a very small list of mainland American casualties during the war from enemy activity.

!!!
Bat Bombs

Natural scientists may be fascinated by them, but in folklore and even today's occult world, bats are associated with death, vampirism and Count Dracula himself. A dentist from Pennsylvania, Lytle S. Adams, saw a new role for them in January 1942 when he sent a written proposal to Franklin D. Roosevelt's White House. The concept was to drop bats fitted with tiny incendiary devices onto Japanese cities, giving the animals enough time to find a building to roost in. It was estimated by experts that a bat bomb could cause ten times as many fires as an ordinary bomb, with no loss of life unlike conventional bomber units.

Adams knew Eleanor Roosevelt, the formidable wife of the President and she persuaded her husband to take the dentist's nonsense seriously. The National Research Defense Committee, headed for this project by Donald Griffin, a famous psychologist, carried out experiments. 'This man is not a nut,' F.D. Roosevelt wrote and Project X-Ray, using Mexican free-tailed bats, took wind in March 1943. Initial tests had mixed results. In one case bats were accidentally released, setting fire to an airbase and a general's car. Two million dollars were spent and then the notion of bat bombs was discarded as the development of the atomic bomb was considered a more effective way to bring the war to an early end.

!
Batmen

Batman, aka millionaire Bruce Wayne, first appeared in #27 of Detective Comics in May 1939, four months before the war began. Developing over the years since, the caped crusader has adapted via the intensely serious world of comics and Hollywood, but could some of his extraordinary powers have been harnessed for real?

The element of surprise is one of a soldier's greatest weapons, and what could be more surprising than a regiment of winged soldiers gliding down silently from the sky? This was the idea of Major Malcolm Wheeler-Nicholson of the California State Guard. Nicholson was the brains behind DC Comics, for which Batman was created and had served as an officer with the 9th cavalry, the Buffalo Soldiers, before serving as an envoy in Russia and Japan. When his military career nose-dived, he began writing lurid pulp fiction to make ends meet. But Wheeler-Nicholson never fully abandoned a serious interest in things military and made sure, via his many useful contacts, that prototypes and testing began, with the hope that eventually all paratroopers could be equipped with jump suits fitted with diving wings, in addition to their parachutes which would be deployed later, that could then be controlled to dodge and weave enemy fire as they descended. Practicalities and lack of cash got in the way and the plans were abandoned but the concepts put forward are still used by skydivers to this day.

!

The Battle of Los Angeles

After Pearl Harbor the Americans didn't know what Japan would throw at them next. The only direct air raid on the American mainland to cause any death or injury took place at Ellwood, near Santa Barbara, California on the night of 23 February, 1942. The next night one of Los Angeles' strangest incidents happened. The air raid sirens began to sound out and a black out was enforced. Air Raid Wardens dashed into action. Ed Murrow and other reporters based in London had been broadcasting regularly to American cities and everyone was on high alert, expecting aerial bombardment by the Japanese, mirroring the Luftwaffe's Blitz over England. The anti-aircraft guns fired off over 1,500 rounds into the night sky and sporadic firing continued for nearly an hour. The 'All Clear' finally sounded at 7.21am. Five civilians died – three in car crashes in the chaos of the alarm and two others from heart attacks

This 'battle' remains controversial to this day. The Secretary of the Navy, Frank Knox, said the following day 'it was a false alarm' and no enemy aircraft was shot down or spotted. Despite this, newspapers cried out that it was a cover up and there are a large number of people today who believe it was in fact a UFO, a theme that would capture the imaginations of Americans in the following decades.

Experts believe it was a combination of a stray air balloon, shaky nerves and that the barrage simply followed the first shot. The public's reaction to the government's official response may be the first time that Americans began to doubt the integrity of their leaders.

!

'Bavarian' Joe

Scandalous cases of sexual impropriety do not belong exclusively to our own time. One of them may have removed an obstacle to Hitler's path to the war. 'Bavarian' Joe was actually a Berliner, Otto Schmidt, a career criminal and low-life who specialised in blackmailing male celebrities. The Nazi leadership, many of whom were notorious for their heterosexual flings, frowned on homosexuality and it emerged that Schmidt had had an encounter in the toilets of a Potsdam railway station with Colonel General Werner Freiherr von Fritsch, commander of the Wehrmacht, in 1933.

There had been a file on all this submitted by Richard Heydrich, in his position as head of the Reich Security service, the SD. At first, Hitler purported not to believe it, but the fact was that von Fritsch was an old-school soldier, appalled by Hitler's headlong rush to a war that he was convinced Germany was not ready for. Von Fritsch was in the way. The Gestapo interrogated him on 27 January 1938 and he was confronted by Schmidt, brought from Börgermoor internment camp for the purpose. He claimed that, in the Potsdam encounter, von Fritsch had smoked a cigarette (he had given up smoking in 1925); wore a fur coat (he never owned one) and told the lad he was commander of the army (a role he was not given until a year later). Despite the arrant nonsense spouted by Schmidt, von Fritsch did the honourable thing and resigned.

He was recalled to the army just before the outbreak of war and was killed near Warsaw, Poland, on 22 September 1939. It was generally believed at the time that he had done this deliberately.

!

Beefsteak Nazis

Within the political ideologies that contended in Europe in the 1920s and '30s, Fascism and Communism dominated. The Bolshevik Revolution in 1917 terrified the west who saw their long-held interest in capitalism under attack. To combat the Red threat, Fascism became the order of the day, accepted in Germany, Italy and Spain by the 1930s, but the way there was strewn with corpses, from street fighting in German cities to all-out civil war in Spain.

Even within Hitler's Nazi party there were shades of opinion. One of these was spearheaded by the Strasser brothers, Gregor and Otto, who advocated a more radical, working class strand of National Socialism. These people were contemptuously called 'beefsteak Nazis' – brown on the outside (the colour of the SA uniform) and red inside (the colour of the Communist flag).

When the Russian army was closing in on Germany by late 1944, there is evidence that some of these men tried to defect to them. The *Daily Press* (California) of 22 September said,

> 'Their change will fool nobody. Like some beefsteaks, they will probably be done to a turn.'

!
The Bellamy Salute

The extending of the right arm out with a flat hand will now always belong to the shadow of the Fascists, but it wasn't always theirs. American schoolchildren throughout the country had been doing it every day for decades and no one thought anything of it. Both the Fascist and the American versions probably stem from the ancient Roman salute given to emperors, superior officers and legionary standards, although we are not exactly sure what form this took.

In an act of fervent patriotism in 1892, a magazine owner named Daniel Sharp Ford set out on his mission to get a US flag in every classroom and with the American Civil War still in living memory, this was seen as a unifying gesture. Sharp asked one of his writers, the Christian Socialist minister Francis Bellamy, to come up with a form of words that could be recited by the children. He wrote 'The Pledge of Allegiance' which was extremely popular and was soon being spoken by millions of students - 'I pledge allegiance to my Flag and the Republic for which it stands; one Nation indivisible, with Liberty and Justice for all.'

Sharp and Bellamy thought something was missing, and a salute was necessary to complement the words, so they advised all young patriots to stretch out their right hand, slightly upwards in the direction of the flag. The Bellamy salute began to make people uncomfortable by the 1930s and the identical salute of the Fascists in Europe raised many concerns. As relations between the US and Germany became hostile, leading to outright war in December 1941, a law was passed a year later replacing the Bellamy salute with the right hand instead being placed over the heart. The ultra-traditional Daughters of the American Revolution resisted at first, but eventually fell into line with everybody else.

!!!

The Bitch of Buchenwald

The appalling story of torture, medical experiments and extermination carried out by the Reich between 1933 and 1945 defies description. Many of the anecdotes in this book are intentionally light-hearted. Humour, especially in beleaguered Britain, was a vital psychological release. But the behaviour of some individuals goes far beyond weird and the career of Ilse Koch, the 'bitch of Buchenwald' is a prime example. The original version was 'witch' (hexe) but the alliteration of the other version took hold and is the one used today.

She married SS Standartenfuhrer (Colonel) Karl-Otto Koch at an open air ceremony in 1936 and three years later the couple were posted to the concentration camp at Buchenwald, he as commandant, she as an SS Helferinnen (assistant). The Nazi mindset did not allow women to told important posts in any capacity – something else that is weird by today's standards. While he made a small fortune out of his exalted position (in direct opposition to the ideals of integrity preached by Heinrich Himmler as head of the SS) Ilse became known as a nymphomaniac with marked sadistic tendencies.

For decade the assumption was made that *all* Nazis had these vicious tendencies which explains the Holocaust in the first place, but Ilse went beyond the 'norms' of abnormality. She was obsessed with tattooed skin and had the skin of camp inmates removed from corpses and made into lampshades, gloves and wallets. She continued working even after her husband was hanged by the Reich early in 1945 and came to trial two years later.

Found guilty of murder, she was sentenced to life imprisonment. Extraordinarily, this was reduced by US General Lucius Clay (who believed that the lampshades were made of goatskin) to four years. In October 1949, she was released, only to be re-arrested for incitement to murder. The Senate examined her war record and she was re-tried in 1951. The decision of the court on the advice of psychiatrists was that she was a 'perverted, nymphomaniacal, power-mad demon'. In prison for life, she seduced an American army warder and gave birth. She hanged herself in Ailsach prison in September 1967.

Just as weird as Ilse, perhaps more so, is the series of Nazi exploitation films featuring sadism, blood and lesbianism produced particularly in Italy and France throughout the 1970s and '80s. The best known, *Ilsa, the She Wolf of the SS* and clearly based on Koch, was made in Canada in 1974.

Slightly less well known than Ilse is Irma Grese, the Belle of Auschwitz, also known as the Blonde Angel of Hell. She became a camp guard at the age of twenty-one and spent hours whipping inmates and gloating over medical experiments carried out by doctors such as Josef Mengele, the Angel of Death, with whom she may have had an affair. Another lover was probably the commandant of Bergen-Belsen, Josef Kramer. Found guilty of war crimes, she was hanged by Albert Pierrepoint. Staring him in the face, she simply said, '*Schnell*!' (quick!).

!
The Black Devil

Erich Hartmann was a *Luftwaffe* fighter pilot and holds the record as the world's top flying ace with the highest recorded number of kills, earning himself the nickname 'The Black Devil' among the Soviets and the slightly less intimidating 'Bubi' (young boy) from his comrades. He is here not because he was weird but because his kill-list is so extraordinary. His nickname (Chemiy Chort in Russian) comes from the black tulip design on his engine cowling.

Erich's mother was a glider pilot (one of the first in Germany) and set up her own flying school, within which Erich became an instructor at the age of fourteen! Joining the *Luftwaffe* in 1940 he was extremely confident in his own abilities and a stunt where he performed aerobatics showing off over the Zerbst airfield saw him literally grounded and losing two thirds of his pay. This hubris may have saved his life as a friend was killed the same afternoon flying a Messerschmitt Bf109 that should have been Hartmann's.

Despite a rocky start to his career, 'Bubi' would go on to take part in over 1,400 combat missions, shooting down an unbeatable 352 enemy planes. He dodged death and crash landed fourteen times, always due to mechanical failure not enemy action.

What made Hartmann such a killing machine in the air? His philosophy was 'get close [to within 66 feet or less] – when the enemy fills the entire windscreen you can't miss.' He was deadly at stalk and ambush tactics and believed that 80 per cent of the pilots he shot down had literally no idea what hit them.

Hartmann surrendered his I/JG52 unit to the American 90th Division and was handed over to the Soviets. He was tried on trumped up charges of war crimes and convicted, serving ten of his twenty-five-year sentence before being released in 1955. This conviction has since been quashed as a 'malicious prosecution.' The Black Devil became a civilian flight instructor and lived peacefully to the age of seventy-one.

!!
The Blitz Witch

Helen Duncan was a Scottish medium and clairvoyant who operated during the war. Born to a working class Presbyterian family in Callander, Perthshire, in 1897, she gravitated from teenage hysteria to full blown 'spirit contact' during the 1920s. The mother of six gave séances to people, claiming to be able to speak to the recently departed. The Victorians had loved this cross between spiritualism and parlour trickery and the number of dead in the First World war made séances popular again as bereaved families tried desperately to contact their dear departed. During her performances Helen would have nosebleeds and produce ectoplasm from her mouth, which was actually a mixture of cheesecloth and paper and cuttings from magazines. Tests conducted by British experts on psychic phenomena were not supportive to Helen, to put it mildly. The Society for Psychical Research were not impressed.

Photographs taken in 1928 reveal the various manifestations as laughable. Faces from magazines have clearly been stuck on to lavatory paper in some of them. The 'ghost hunter' Harry Price concluded, 'Could anything be more infantile than a group of grown-up men wasting time, money and energy on the antics of a fat, female crook?' Despite this public humiliation and a number of prosecutions and fines, Helen carried on her work and during a séance in Portsmouth in November 1941, she revealed that HMS *Barham* had been sunk and that she was talking to one of the dead sailors named Sid. The sinking of the *Barham* was not revealed by the government until January 1942 so Intelligence officers began to watch her more closely. Two Naval officers attended a séance in 1944 and were not impressed by her powers though and reported her to the police. Although the loss of *Barham* had not been revealed to the public, the families of the 861 dead had been informed in private so there is no reason to believe she couldn't have found that information out from them and the wartime rumour machine. Winston Churchill's government, via the Ministry of Information, continued the poster paranoia that 'careless talk costs lives' and 'tittle-tattle lost the battle' but the need for secrecy often ran counter to human nature.

The government nevertheless deemed the 'Blitz Witch' a security risk and decided to charge her for various offences so she appeared in court. Duncan and her defence team offered to conduct a séance in the court but this was declined by the jury. She was found guilty and sentenced to be imprisoned for nine months at Holloway, London's female prison. She was originally to be charged for espionage and treason but astonishingly was convicted under Clause 4 of the Witchcraft Act of 1735! 'I have done nothing,' she shouted from the dock. 'Is there a God?'

According to some reports the prison wardens refused to lock Helen's cell and had readings from her. Her séances in front of paying customers seem harmless enough. For a person to be imprisoned in twentieth century Britain as a witch says much about the paranoia of the leaders of the country at the time, although Churchill himself believed the trial was a farcical waste of time and angrily described her charge in a letter to the Home Secretary, Herbert Morrison, as 'obsolete tomfoolery.' Duncan continued to be harassed by the government until her death in 1956. The Witchcraft Act of 1735 was repealed in 1951. In 2012 the Scottish government rejected a petition to pardon her. 'Hellish Nell' remains Britain's last convicted witch.

!
The Blood Flag

Die Blutfahne (the Blood Flag) was a Nazi flag that took on an almost sacred quality and was treated like a martyr's relic. The original *blutbannr* was a scarlet flag associated with Medieval states and carried by the German *landsknechte*, mercenaries of the sixteenth century. Hitler's version was that of the 6th SA (*Sturmabteilung*) and was carried by Heinrich Trambauer in November 1923 during the Beer Hall Putsch in Munich, a failed attempt to wrest power from the Communist government. Sixteen Nazis and four policemen died in the violence that ensued. One of the brown shirts, Andreas Bauriedl, was killed and fell onto the flag, staining it with his blood. As the SA fled, one of them took the flag from its staff and stuffed it in his jacket, hiding it away for safekeeping. After serving nine months in prison for his attempted coup, Hitler was given the flag.

Upon receiving it, Hitler had a new staff made and the names of the sixteen brown shirts who died carved into its silver sleeve. *Die Blutfahne* was given to the SS in 1926, after which it took part in Nazi ceremonies, being used to touch other flags to 'sanctify' them as part of a flag consecration ceremony. The flag was housed in the Brown House, the Nazi headquarters in Munich and had an SS guard of honour. Although the glorifying of the dead of the Beer Hall was out of all proportion to what they achieved, the notion of standards as holy relics had a very ancient pedigree, stretching back to the Romans and beyond.

The flag's last known use was on 18 October 1944 after which it disappears from record. It is likely the flag was simply destroyed when the Headquarters were bombed by the Allies, or, at a push, it may have been taken to a place of safety. Either way, the holy relic of the Reich has never been seen since.

!!
Board Games for the Reich

The lengths the Nazi leadership went to in order to control the minds of their subjects is overwhelming. As part of their total war for the hearts and minds of Germany, they even made children's board games!

Jagd auf Kohlenklau (Hunting for the Coal Thief) was a game designed in 1944 and was used to encourage energy conservation as part of the German war effort. The war economy was driven by Hitler's architect Albert Speer and the speed of war production was astonishing. The game sees players move across fifty squares trying to avoid landing on tiles such as 'left the radio on, miss a turn.' This continues until one of them is declared the winner, thus 'evicting the coal thief'.

The idea of the game is quite benign, compared with two other games made by private companies during the Nazi regime. *Bomber über England* (Bomber over England) was a pinball style game where players would try to direct the ball to holes on a map of Britain, representing key cities, while trying to avoid having their 'bombs' land harmlessly in the North Sea. Players lose points for 'bombing' areas of the Reich.

The most baffling and wicked game to come out of the age has to be the 1936 creation of *Juden Raus!* (Jews Out!) by Gunther & Co. In this board game, playing pieces were pointed hats, representing Jews. Players are then in a race with their opponents to move all of their Jews out of the city and deport them to Palestine before anyone else. Surprisingly, the SS were not impressed by this game, believing it trivialized the Jewish 'problem'. Ironically, the SS solution to the 'problem' was more absurd then the objective of the children's game. Though it would be unfair to blame any child for enjoying a board game without an understanding of its deeper meaning, it is still uncomfortable to picture German families sitting down together playing it.

!
The Bollocks of the Blitz

There is no doubt that *the* defining experience of the Peoples' War was the series of bombing raids on British cities in 1940-41 which were visited on German cities by the RAF and the USAAF in 1944-45. The aim of both was to terrify and demoralize the civilian population, forcing their governments to surrender. And, in both cases, it was an abject failure.

In an attempt to outwit the enemy during night-time attacks (raids in the daytime were quickly discovered to be suicidal) a blackout was imposed and the cry 'Put that light out' became a stock catchphrase. Men let their white shirts hang out of their trousers to aid travel on the darkened streets and kerb stones were painted white. Even so, road accidents rocketed in number, at a time when nobody owned a car and journeys were restricted because of petrol rationing. The London firm of Marshall and Snelgrove sold white coats for the dogs of the upper classes and private detectives had their work cut out in divorce cases. 'Adultery,' noted *Reynolds News* in January 1940, 'cannot be proved because identification is impossible in the pitch dark.'

The Blitz, first in London, then in the provincial centres like Coventry, Hull, Plymouth, Liverpool and Sheffield, killed thousands and destroyed property on an unprecedented scale. The sights and sounds and smells that the overstretched rescue services had to witness were often beyond belief. Even so, a grim battle humour shone through, from East Enders 'who could take it' to the bombed House of Commons itself. On 8 October 1940, Churchill told the House that given the rate of bombing and the hit-rate of the Luftwaffe, it would take ten years for half of London's houses to be demolished. 'After that, of course, progress would be much slower.'

The rumour machine kicked in big time. Someone saw a Zeppelin shot down over Essex. Refugees from bombed cities were causing a massive increase in venereal disease among those generous enough to take them in. In London, two million dogs and cats were put down because of a government order – and this was in the first week of the war, long before the Blitz started. When Merseyside was badly hit in May 1941, stories abounded of martial law in the area, train loads of burned corpses carried to the crematoria, rioting was widespread and thousands had taken to the streets carrying white flags of truce and demanding an end to it all. None of this actually happened. People *did* complain, not unnaturally. One London borough put in an official complaint because the reverberation of the anti-aircraft batteries was cracking lavatory seats in council houses.

As early as August 1940, before provincial raids started at all, more than seventy German parachutes were found in the Midlands, 'proof' of an invasion. Luftwaffe pilots and crew shot down over England wore rouge and lipstick. 'The medical profession,' sneered the *Daily Mirror* of 16 April 1941, 'has a word for men of this type. It classifies them as moral deviants …' No one was too surprised by this. Anybody who could bring such terror from the skies could hardly be normal.

Various reports, all unsubstantiated, told a shell-shocked public that a pilot who bailed out over the East End was torn to pieces by the mob.

And if it weren't so grim, the Blitz had its comic side. A number of East End families swore they emerged from the Tubes and other shelters to find that the only part of their house still standing was the front door; it usually had the pet dog, completely unharmed of course, still tied to the door knob! One lady in Mayfair was rocketed out into the street in her bath. Others were sitting on the loo. Whole cities became beyond exhausted by night after night of raids and sales of Horlicks for 'deep, healing sleep' rocketed. When Madame Tussaud's was hit, some of its inhabitants were scattered along Marylebone Road like so many corpses.

Humour of course came to the rescue. A cardboard, hand written sign outside a shattered London police station read, 'Be good; we're still open!' Shops with no fronts put up signs reading, 'More open than usual'. Others just wrote, 'Blast!' One pub caught the mood of defiance perfectly – 'Our windows are gone but our spirits are excellent. Come in and try them.'

The shelters themselves became little microcosms of the

shattered world above, offering sing-songs, stand-up comedians and, in the case of cinemas, as many as five feature films a night. The Blitz mentality saw a camaraderie unknown before the war and unknown since. The fact that it was engendered by fear did not lessen its importance. It cut across barriers of class, race, education and upbringing. Strange superstitions kicked in. The Germans never bombed the same house twice; in one London borough, everybody wanted a local Nigerian as their Air Raid Precautions warden because his black face was less of a target! When Plymouth was hit, several locals swore they heard the beating of Drake's drum, as though their sixteenth century hero had come to save them.

Cities began to look like deserted battlefields and the scars would last for years. The ubiquitous rosebay willow herb that grew on bomb sites came to be called fireweed. Those whose houses had been hit had the additional embarrassment that passers-by on their way to work could see their bedroom wallpaper and would, at the very least, raise eyebrows of disapproval at their lack of taste.

People died. Homes were smashed. The country was brought to breaking point. But it did not break. And the tide of war swept on in a different direction.

!!

The Bombing of Brookings

In the early stages of the Pacific War, Japan's obvious problem was how to contain America's powerful fleet. The answer was to cause havoc at home and force the US navy to return to its own waters for defence.

Nobuo Fujita was a pilot in the Japanese Imperial Navy who carried out the second – and last – continental aircraft bombing on the United States. He and his crewman, Shoji Okuda, flew from a 1-25 submarine that surfaced off the Oregon coast near the town of Brookings, Oregon in 1942. His mission was to use his seaplane to drop incendiary bombs to start forest fires. The damage was minimal and a second sortie was barely noticed. Fujita's one man bombing campaign of continental America was a failure.

Despite this, twenty years later, the terror of the skies was invited back. He was assured by his own government in 1962 he was not going to be tried as a war criminal so accepted the invitation. In an act of honourable remorse, Fujita gave his family's 400-year-old samurai sword to the Americans as a gift. He intended to use the sword to commit *seppuku* (honourable suicide) if he was unwelcome; happily, the people of Brookings forgave him and he was declared an honorary citizen in 1990.

Fujita became an unofficial ambassador for peace, inviting students to Japan and he even received a letter from the office of President Ronald Reagan in admiration of his kindness and generosity. In the last years of his life he planted a tree at the bombing site as a gesture of peace and some of his ashes are scattered on Mount Emily, which he had pointlessly bombed fifty-five years earlier.

!
The Bride of Belsen

Gena Turgel was a Polish survivor of the nightmare that was Bergen-Belsen concentration camp. She lost all of her family was sent to Auschwitz. That camp has become synonymous with the barbarity of the Third Reich and remains today a museum and shrine to its millions of victims. As the Red Army was closing in she then endured a forced march to Bergen-Belsen. These 'death marches' served no purpose, as there was no safe place now for the remnants of Hitler's regime. Thousands died on the roads and in the ghastly cattle trucks, moving from camp to camp. Gena shared a barracks with Anne Frank, the most famous of all concentration camp victims, thanks to the diary she kept while in hiding during the German occupation of the Netherlands. The camp was liberated in April 1945 and the appalling conditions there, reported by Richard Dimbleby for the BBC, shocked the world. For most this was their first experience of how terrible the Holocaust was.

Through the unimaginable horror of it all, there was still some hope. A young British soldier named Norman Turgel was one of the first to come across the camp and took part in the overwhelming task of saving as many people as they could. Gena was starving and in rags. He immediately said, 'This is the girl I am going to marry.' He then helped bundle the vicious camp commandant, Josef Kramer, into a cell, looking into his face and telling him, 'I am a Jew.' Norman fell in love with Gena and proposed to her several days later. She said yes.

Her wedding dress was made from a silk parachute and she went to Britain with Turgel in October, being labelled by the press 'The Bride of Belsen.' Gena and Norman had a happy life, with three children. She spent several years telling British school children about her experiences. Of the inmates of Belsen, she said, 'They were ordinary people like you and they were murdered for no reason.'

!

The Brothers of the Forest

Operation Barbarossa, the German invasion of the USSR instantly turned Russia from an enemy to an ally. From 1941 to '45, Britain regarded Russia as a friend, sending vital supplies via North Sea convoys. The reality, for the states of Estonia, Latvia and Lithuania, is that the Red menace was every bit as deadly as the Nazi occupation. While the world focussed on the evils of Hitler, most people beyond his grasp ignored the equal evils of 'Uncle Joe' Stalin. So, for many countries, their 'liberation' from Nazi Germany wasn't really a liberation at all. After the war, while France and West Germany were celebrating the return of democracy, countries like Lithuania, Ukraine and Poland simply had one form of foreign dictatorship replaced with another. In fact, their liberators were the same people who had conquered them before retreating from the Nazis in 1939.

Stalin's rule of the Baltic states was cruel and totalitarian; over one hundred thousand people would die in fighting and reprisals in the years to come. Tens of thousands joined the 'Forest Brothers', groups of guerrilla fighters that hid from their enemy in the vast forests of their nations in 1940. The partisans suffered heavy losses and were no match for the Red Army, so their tactics resorted to small cells conducting ambushes. Torture and death awaited any captured Forest Brothers whose mantra was 'save the last bullet for yourself.' For these countries, the war did not end in 1945 and Stalin's men were no different from Hitler's. The Soviet Union would continue to occupy the Baltic states until 1991.

!!
Busy Lizzie

Nazi scientists were busy throughout the war (as were their Allied counterparts) trying to perfect more deadly weapons than the enemy. The V1 and V2 rockets – 'doodlebugs' – brought a new Blitz to British cities in 1944 and the V3 (*Vergeltungswaffe* 3) was a development of this technology. It was considered a 'revenge weapon'. Built on the northern coast of France, this huge cannon had barrels that were over 400ft long and was claimed to be capable of firing 600 shots every hour towards London. For this reason it came to be known as the London Gun, although the pattern of rocket boosters along its barrel gave it its German codename *tausendfussler* (millipede).

As with many Nazi superweapons, it was theoretically possible, but it was a huge drain on resources and manpower that many military commanders' thought was better placed elsewhere. Scientists also doubted the capabilities of the gun to achieve what it was supposed to. Hitler's obsession meant the plan was to go ahead, but thanks to the work of the RAF's 617 Squadron (the Dambusters), the cannon was damaged by aerial bombardment and put out of action.

The Nazis still had hopes for this weapon, even after D-Day. One of the four V3 cannons was relocated to Germany and used to bombard Luxembourg. The weapon that was meant to change the war was not impressive; a month long bombardment killed only ten people. In the end, time ran out and the German railway network was so damaged by Allied bombing that it was impossible to provide ammunition for the 'Busy Lizzie' as the gun was ironically called. The Americans captured all superweapons they could find and sent them to the US for testing, before giving up on this one in 1948.

!!
The Carpet Chewer

The German word is *teppichfresser* and it was a term of contempt applied to Hitler by non-Nazis. To explain the extraordinary rise of the Fuhrer and the hold he had over millions, we have to factor in his explosive temper. How much of this was the genuine bitterness of a sociopath and how much part of his public persona is difficult to tell. He certainly screamed and ranted if he thought he could get his way – he did it at the Munich Conference in 1938 and most of his cleverly crafted speeches ended on an hysterical note. This led some people to make assumptions. Birgir Dahlerus, a Swedish diplomat, found him 'patently unstable'. Neville Henderson, the British ambassador in Berlin before the war, said he was 'quite mad', having 'crossed the borderline of insanity'. Manfred Schroder, a Nazi underling who was with Hitler at the time of Munich, described him as 'an absolute maniac'.

If he behaved like a spoiled child with tantrums, there is no doubt that it often worked in that he got his way and minions were genuinely afraid of him, especially if they had to be the bearers of bad news.

There is no evidence that he ever rolled on the ground, frothing at the mouth and literally chewing the carpet with rage as the nickname suggests, but the same behaviour is ascribed to King John of England, who gnawed at the floor covering at Windsor Castle having been forced to put his seal to Magna Carta in 1215. The problem with *that* story is that in John's day, carpets were tapestries and hung from the walls; the floor was covered in straw.

!!
Carrots

It was believed that carrots could help you see in the dark. At a stretch there is a truth to this; if you have a Vitamin A deficiency you will develop nyctalopia and carrots help but only to the point of returning your eyes to a normal level. The myth was useful however to the British Air Ministry. In an effort to keep the Germans in the dark as to their recent development of radar, they claimed that the Royal Air Force pilots were being fed carrots to give them night vision and thereby explain why they were quick to find and intercept the *Luftwaffe* on bombing raids. The story focussed on Group Captain John 'Cats' Eyes' Cunningham of 604 Squadron who shot down an enemy aircraft in December 1940 with radar aid.

The public certainly believed it and the myth gave renewed impetus to the Ministry of Food and the 'grow your own' campaign – 'Dig For Victory'.

Carrots of course were the least of it. As rationing became the norm and food supplies dwindled, the public had to make do with substitutes of all kinds. Powdered egg, whale meat, 'snoek' (tinned fish) and much later, Spam, all joined the carrots and turnips of Woolton Pie. Even Christmas puddings had a high vegetable content. The BBC broadcast *The Kitchen Front*, advocated the use of spaghetti and noodles. Most housewives had never heard of these and some refused to buy them because they were foreign and Britain was at war with the Italians.

!!!

The Case of the Deadly Double

It sounds like a Perry Mason television episode (in fact it was, in 1958!) but this particular double had more sinister and more serious connotations. Two weeks before the Japanese attack on Pearl Harbor, advertisements appeared in the *New Yorker* magazine for a dice game. To draw readers' attention to it, the words Achtung! Warning! and Alerte! were used – all of them heard all too frequently in war-torn Europe at the time. The dice themselves, tumbling in mid-air, showed a series of numbers on the faces – O, 5, 7, 12, 24 and XX. It purported to be Chicago's favourite game and one that could be played in an air raid shelter (something the Americans would never have to do for real).

The Pearl Harbor attack led to high alerts across America and the FBI became convinced that the Deadly Double game was a code on behalf of the Japanese war machine. 12 and 7 on the dice was the date of the attack; 5 and 0 referred to the time of the raid and XX was 20, the latitude of Pearl. 24 was perhaps the code sign of the agent who had placed the ads. The FBI's investigation revealed that the Deadly Double Game did not exist; neither did the Monarch company that purported to make it. To this day, the case remains unsolved.

!!!
Castle Itter

Five days after Hitler killed himself, the war would see one of its most unusual battles; an alliance of German and American soldiers fighting the SS in Austria to save Frenchmen. Castle Itter, part of the Dachau concentration camp organization, was used to intern many of France's most powerful people including former prime ministers Edouard Daladier and Paul Raynard, ex commanders of the Army Maxime Weygand and Maurice Gamelin and even a famous tennis star, Jean Borotra. In May 1945 the guards fled, fearing execution from the SS; two prisoners set off to find help. They came across a Wehrmacht major, Josef Gangl, opposed to the Nazis and working with the Austrian resistance. As he only had twenty men he wasn't able to provide an adequate defence. Under the truce of a white flag, Gangl met up with the 23rd Tank Battalion of the US XXI Corps, led by Captain Jack Lee and explained the situation to him. Lee agreed to help defend the castle.

The men took up defensive positions and waited for the inevitable attack. On 5 May a 150 strong unit of the 17th Panzergrenadier Division, Waffen SS attacked the castle and blew up a tank and laid siege. Captain Lee was able to radio for help and reinforcements were dispatched, but the communication was intercepted before it was completed. So tennis star Borotra vaulted the castle walls, survived the gunfire of the encircling enemy and met up with the relief force. Borotra was an old hand at escapes – this was his third in two years. The defenders were almost out of ammunition and made plans to fall back to the keep and fight hand to hand if necessary but fortunately their back-up arrived in the late afternoon. Over 100 SS soldiers were taken prisoner. The only casualty among the defenders was Josef Gangl, who was killed by a sniper while protecting Paul Reynaud. Today, he is considered an Austrian hero. Germany would surrender within three days.

!!!
Cat Bombs

The aircraft carrier was undoubtedly a war-winning weapon of the Second World War, but its technology was hugely demanding. A pilot had to take off from the deck of a moving ship, find an enemy ship and drop his bombs on it before returning to the mother ship. Everything is moving – sea, ship, plane, bombs – a nightmare of physics. So the American Office of Strategic Services, forerunner of the CIA, dreamed up the cat bomb. Because cats hate water and because they have an uncanny ability to land on their feet, the idea was to drop cats attached with bombs from the air onto naval targets. As the cats landed in the water they would instinctively head towards the vessels and thus detonate their explosive. This idea never got passed the testing stages as the cats would lose consciousness on their descent. Quite how the cats could have swum after a ship with a bomb attached to them in an open ocean was another imponderable of physics and could only be explained by the paranoid geeks of the OSS.

!!
The Channel White with Bodies

In June 1940, Britain stood alone. The army had been driven out of France at Dunkirk and the next military step, it seemed obvious, was the invasion of Britain. It was an extraordinarily difficult thing to do; the last successful invasion by a foreign power took place in 1066. The point was that aerial and bombing technology had added to the terror and several of Churchill's military advisers were telling him that Germany would be bound to win the war.

In August as the Battle of Britain raged in the skies over southern Britain, there were reports of a parachute landing in the north and constant rumours that the Isle of Wight, like Jersey and Guernsey, had already been overrun by the Wehrmacht. By Christmas, America, still not in the war, was reporting in various newspapers that two German invasions had been repulsed with a loss of 80,000 men; so many that their corpses gave the Channel a whitish appearance and were being washed up all along the south coast. French hospitals were choked with wounded and the Channel itself blazed with burning oil. And none of this was true.

There were indeed casualties from an invasion scare, but they were British, not German. Reports of a Kriegsmarine break out from the Dutch coast prompted the 20th Destroyer Flotilla of the Royal Navy to investigate. They ran into a minefield, two ships were sunk and a third was damaged. The wounded were brought back to various hospitals along the east coast and the government probably believed that a rumour about a scotched invasion would sound better than a failed raid.

In early September another 'invasion' was foiled, at Sandwich Bay in Kent. This time the water was *black* with German dead, rather than white. The majority of British people had never seen a German in uniform and believed (as many people still do) that the Wehrmacht wore the Waffen SS's black uniforms, rather than the field grey they actually wore. Similar landings were reported to have happened in the west country and in Scotland; there were thousands of dead on Clacton beach alone. Some of these corpses were apparently tied up in groups of three; as diarist James Hudson noted, with or without a straight face, 'Lots of funny stories go about.' At Southend, the bodies were supposedly picked up by council rubbish lorries.

Wing-commander Guy Gibson, who led 617 Squadron's famous raid on the Mohne and Eide dams in 1943 summed up the situation very well – 'no one will ever know anyone who saw a dead German soldier, although many a man will claim to know someone else who knows someone else who buried one.'

In May 1940, AP Herbert, poet, MP and member of the Naval Reserve, called for calm –

'Do not believe the tale the milkman tells;
No troops have mutinied at Potters Bar,
Nor are there submarines at Tunbridge Wells.
The BBC will warn us when there are.'

In fact, it was in the interests of Churchill's government to give invasion rumours their head. What is common to them all is that the corpses were *German* – in other words, the invasion failed. Blitzkrieg was beaten back. This positive ethos was exactly what Churchill wanted in his desperate bid to bring the Americans into the war – Britain was far from beaten, but a little help would be nice. The icing on the cake of these stories was the weapons technology actually going on in Britain at the time – and of course, top secret – which let the world believe that they could stave off invasion for ever by setting fire to the sea.

!!

Churchill's Toyshop

Churchill's Toyshop was the nickname for the top secret British laboratory MD1, itself part of the secret weapons development unit MI9, attached to Military Intelligence Research run by Lt. Colonel Joe Holland of the Royal Engineers. Originally based in the cellars of Radio Normandie in Portland Place, London, MD1 relocated after being bombed, to a Buckinghamshire mansion called The Firs near Aylesbury. Even – perhaps especially – during a war, the various government ministries fell over each other, bickering as to exactly who did what; and inevitably, it was all about funding. Churchill was keen to cut through the red tape and his War Cabinet controlled everything that MD1 did.

The list of inventions – some brilliant, others silly – have filled whole books and this snippet can only scratch the surface. They included the Limpet Mine, used to sink enemy ships, which contained condoms and aniseed balls as part of its components. Another invention was the sticky bomb, of which the prototype involved porridge. Churchill was impressed and told them 'Sticky bomb – make one million.' Containing nitro-glycerine, they were stuck to vehicles and were used extensively by commando units. Time pencils were delayed detonator fuses. M mines were made of cardboard. The 'Bomb, H.E. Ainslie, Aircraft, JW' was the 'Johnnie Walker', designed to travel underwater until it reached the keel of a ship, when it would explode. L-Delay fuses also allowed bomb fuses to be lit, with a delay on the explosion of over a week! The huge numbers of uncanny inventions made by the team was probably author Ian Fleming's inspiration for his character Q in the James Bond novels. Fleming was with Naval Intelligence during the war.

!

The Code Talkers

In any war, there is a need for secrecy and government departments have been set up with that specifically in mind. They usually operated complicated systems of code, from Thomas Phelippes working for Sir Francis Walsingham, Elizabeth I's spymaster in the sixteenth century to the elaborate enigma device of the Second World War. But any code, no matter how complex, can be cracked. An actual *language* is infinitely more complicated.

In the United States, the Navajo code talkers are much celebrated heroes of the war and perhaps the most famous code talkers of all, their language being indecipherable to the enemy. The Navajo system was never broken by the Axis powers and they have even been immortalized in the 2002 movie *Windtalkers*. This wasn't the first use of Native Americans; as early as the First World War, the Americans realized they could use the various languages of their First Nations' soldiers to confound their enemies. The Cherokee and Choctaw soldiers were deployed in various roles in the Great War, the first use of Cherokee at the second Battle of the Somme in 1918. The US military continued to use Native American code talkers up to the Vietnam War, utilizing the languages of the Assiniboine, Comanche, Meskwaki and Seminole tribes. The Americans also used their European ancestry, employing descendants of the Basques from northern Spain. The British occasionally used Welsh!.

!
Comfort Women

Throughout history, the 'brutal and licentious soldiery' have assumed a natural right to help themselves to local women, be they the enemy or camp followers. During the war, the Japanese imperial government forced women into sexual slavery for use by their troops in any country they occupied. The estimates for the number of girls coerced into military prostitution varies significantly between 20,000 and 400,000, based on the opinion of different scholars, Japanese and Chinese.

Women from any occupied country were at risk of coming to the attention of the Japanese soldiers but Korea and China appear to be the worst affected. Imperial troops would try to lure girls with promises of work and safety, but the girls ended up finding themselves in 'comfort stations'. If tempting them didn't work, they would simply be stolen from the streets, on one occasion even setting up a girls' school – the Huimi school in occupied China – with the specific intent of abusing the students. Disturbingly, the justification for this was that it would encourage soldiers not to rape indiscriminately. Three out of four comfort women, due to the horrific abuse they received from dozens of men daily, would not survive the war.

The subject remains controversial today with many apologists claiming that the women involved were volunteers. The Japanese government caused outrage in 2016 when their deputy Prime Minister claimed 'there were no documents confirming that the Japanese government or army forced comfort women into sexual servitude', despite previously admitting their role in the 1990s. Less than fifty of these women are still alive today, affectionately called *hadmoni* (grandmothers). Japan has set up a fund to offer these women financial assistance. At the close of the war, only eleven soldiers would be convicted of crimes against women.

!
Comics for the Kids

There was even space for comics in the Nazi propaganda repertoire. The *Vica* was created in occupied France in 1940 to demonize the Allies. Only three issues appear to have been produced. The hero of the comics was a character who looks remarkably like Popeye and the first issue sees him dealing with the British secret service, as well as handling Uncle Sam and Bolshevism.

American children were bombarded too and the sales of comics went towards the war effort from January 1942 onwards. The Nazi hierarchy were invariably shown as aristocratic, with monocles and jackboots; they were always cruel. The Italians were a joke, puppets in the hands of their German masters. The Japanese (clearly *the* unprincipled villains after Pearl Harbor) were portrayed as devious and look like monkeys. Ironically, the all-American heroes, especially Captain America, were often shown as Aryan, with astonishing muscles, blue eyes and blond hair.

In Britain, at least three Fascist leaders were lampooned. The *Dandy* had Addie and Hermie (Hitler and Goering) while the *Beano* had Musso the Wop!

!!
The Confidential Pigeon Service

As with so much from the war years, particularly in the murky realms of the secret services, the truth and scale of the Confidential Pigeon Service is hard to pick out. Author Nigel West wrote 'the whole point about a secret service is that it remains secret' and despite the passing of the Freedom of Information Act in Britain in 2000, a great deal of espionage information is still classified. From 1940 onwards, the British began parachuting pigeons in crates into occupied Europe. Each pigeon was accompanied by writing paper, a special pencil and instructions in various languages; it was then set free to return to their home in London with their message. They were also to have a copy of a London newspaper attached to them, to prove their British origin, although exactly how this was possible is unknown (at least to the present writer!). When Lieutenant John Randall of 1SAS was behind enemy lines in France soon after D-Day, he radioed home to say that a pigeon sent from London had been found, but without the daily paper. He asked whether this was right. Yes, he was told; it was. He sent the pigeon back, but it had not arrived four days later and no one mentioned the bird again.

The phenomenon of pigeons' ability to 'home' is still not completely understood, but is generally accepted to involve the magnetic field of the earth. MI4, who were in charge of the project, were pleased with the results and the intelligence they were receiving. By 1944 the Nazis were so concerned they began deploying their own pigeons, which would home back to the Reich as counter-intelligence, even containing a packet of English cigarettes to fool the receiver.

Thirty-one pigeons received the Dickin Medal for bravery, though they would have to keep that to themselves as our secret pigeon spies did not become public knowledge until the files were released by the National Archives in 2007.

!

The Craziest Pilot

'Beam me up, Scotty,' became one of the best known catchphrases of the 1970s when television's Captain Kirk (William Shatner) of the USS *Enterprise*, gave orders to his chief engineer, Scotty (James Doohan) in *Star Trek*. In fact, Doohan was a genuine war hero of a terrestrial rather than extra-terrestrial war. Joining the Canadian artillery, he was sent to Britain in 1940. His first action as a lieutenant was at Juno Beach on D-Day, killing two snipers. He then led his men through a field of anti-tank mines and was later accidentally shot six times by one of his own men. One bullet hit a finger, which was amputated, four hit his leg, and one hit his chest – the impact of this being stopped by a cigarette case.

Doohan was later attached to the Royal Canadian Air Force and was noted as their 'craziest pilot', once slaloming a Mark IV Auster near RAF Andover between two telegraph poles 'to prove it could be done.'

His death, from pulmonary fibrosis in July 2005, is believed to be related to exposure to toxic substances during the war.

!!
Dawe's D-Day

Leonard Dawe was an old-school headmaster of the Strand School, evacuated to Effingham, Surrey, who submitted more than 5,000 crossword puzzles over the years to the *Daily Telegraph*. Like all British newspapers in wartime, the *Telegraph*'s size was reduced and its news content carefully checked by the authorities. Between 1939 and 1945, Britain came the closest it has ever been to a police state – ironic in that she was fighting against one!

MI5, responsible for espionage and security on the Home Front became suspicious of Dawe's crossword clues. In the spring and summer of 1944, the words 'Utah', 'Gold', 'Sword' and 'Juno' all appeared, as did 'Omaha' – all five were the secret code names for the various beach assaults planned in Operation Overlord, the amphibious landing which came to be called D-Day. Worse followed – on 27 May 'Overlord' itself was a solution and three days later, 'Mulberry' (the floating harbours towed across the Channel to enable landing). On 1 June (five days before the attack) 'Neptune' appeared – the Navy's code name for its part in the assault.

Dawe was interrogated by MI5 but nothing incriminating was found. Two ex-pupils of Dawe have now come forward to say that they had heard those code-names being bandied about by troops stationed near the school in the build-up to D-Day and that it was Dawe's habit to invite boys to help him devise his crossword clues.

While some readers might consider the case closed, that solution is highly unsatisfactory. In a country paranoid to the point of obsession, where 'careless talk costs lives', how feasible is it that squaddies would have known those codes, talked openly about them and that schoolboys would have found the random names so compelling as to pass them on, unwittingly, to Dawe?

!
The Death Match

An American book in 2001 and a Russian film in 2012 have highlighted this bizarre sporting event. As Andy Dougan wrote in 2001, 'If ever soccer was a matter of life and death, then it was here.'

Many of the details of the infamous 'Death Match' are unfortunately hard to unravel due to the layers of legend it has attracted via Soviet propaganda. What is known is that the Ukrainian FC Start, from Kiev, was made up of former professional footballers, now working in an occupied bread factory. On August 6 1942, Start played a *Wehrmacht* team at Zenit Stadium in front of 2,000 people. SS Soldiers and police dogs would have been intimidating to the players, and it was rumoured that the referee was an SS Officer who went into their changing room to tell them to throw the match. He ignored SS fouls and discounted some of Start's goals. These accounts were later denied by the players. FC Start went on to win the match 5 – 1 and the Germans demanded a rematch three days later, which FC Start won again 5 - 3. The Soviet propaganda machine eventually spun their own yarn and the legend grew. Whatever the truth of it, and whether it was linked to football, eight players would soon be arrested by the Gestapo and five would be murdered by the SS within a year.

!!

Degenerate Art Exhibition

One of the apparent enemies of the Reich was modern and abstract art, which must have been culturally threatening to the Nazis. Between July and November 1937 they ran a 'Degenerate Art Exhibition' in Munich showing off 650 works of art they had confiscated.

The idea of this exhibition was to run parallel with an exhibition showing off 'proper' art in the 'Great German Art Exhibition.' Things didn't quite turn out as Hitler and Goebbels had expected; the 'degenerate' exhibition was a raging success with over 2 million people attending, at the same time the 'Great German' exhibition was considered mediocre by critics, with only half the number visiting it.

Hitler saw himself as an artist but his dreams were shattered by his being turned down (twice) by the Viennese School of Art before the First World War. His watercolours, mostly of buildings in Vienna and elsewhere, are not bad, but there is no real creativity or artistry about them. To him, new forms of artistic expression – the new realism of Paul Klee and Wassily Kandinsky – were 'the sick production of crazy people.' There was even a German phrase for this, ironically borrowed from Yiddih, *Meshuggism*, the cult of insanity.

!

The Disloyal Legions

The Free Arabian Legion was the idea of Amin al-Husseini, a Palestinian leader and anti-imperialist. The Legion was to be a *Wehrmacht* unit of Arab volunteers; Palestinians, Iraquis and Tunisians. Al-Husseini led the Arab revolution in Palestine in 1936 and fled the British once they had suppressed it. He hoped to secure the backing of Hitler for an Arab homeland and to overthrow the colonial powers of Britain and France. Hitler agreed to this in 1941 though an attempted overthrow of British rule in Iraq failed. At its height, the unit contained 20,000 men. Sonderverband 287 had three battalions fighting in Tunisia against the Allies' Operation Torch. Others fought in the Balkans.

There is nothing 'free' about those units and, bearing in mind Hitler's obsession with race and the fact that Germany, Italy and Vichy France had occupied all of North Africa, it is difficult to know what the legion thought it would have achieved had Germany won the war. British imperialism would simply have been replaced by the Reich.

The second 'Disloyal Legion' was the Indian, known as the Tiger Legion, a unit within the Wehrmacht, made up of volunteers, Indian POWs and expatriates. The idea was devised by Subhas Chandra Bose, seeking Germany's aid in securing India's independence from the British Empire. Hitler recognized the 'Free India Government' and helped set up a military unit.

The legion reached a maximum size of 3,000 men but they were not deployed in much frontline fighting and most Germans were oblivious. At the close of the war, the Indian Legion attempted to find sanctuary in neutral Switzerland, but were handed over to the Allies, who returned them to India to face charges of treason. Most were released after short prison sentences.

!
The Edelweiss Pirates

Internal opposition to Hitler's Nazis after 1933 was as rare as it was unwise. Those who disagreed with National Socialism and could leave, did so. Others toed the party line. Very few were brave enough to put their heads over the parapet, but, perhaps oddly, some who did were children. Brainwashing of the young was vital if Hitler's Third Reich was to last for a thousand years. Every boy over ten had to join the Hitler Youth (*Hitlerjugend*) run by Baldur von Schirach. Every girl joined the league of German Maidens (*Bund Deutsche Madel*). In both organizations, hearty songs were sung, survival techniques learned and there was total and unswerving devotion to the Fuhrer.

The Edelweiss Pirates were not an organisation as such, but reactionary groups of young German people opposed to Nazi rule and who refused to take part in the Hitler Youth. These disaffected youths, aged between fourteen and seventeen, were anti-authority and the Edelweiss Pirates was a collective term for the various gangs which included groups such as 'The Travelling Dudes' and 'The Navajos' (note the American influence). A loophole in the law meant that they were exempt from the HJ, having left school but were too young for conscription into military service. Their activities were wide ranging but did include anti-Nazi activities, attacks on government officials and sheltering deserters and escaped POWs. At first considered just a nuisance, the Gestapo became suspicious of the Pirates, describing them as 'riff raff – throwing their weight around'.

Punishments for those found to be members were harsh, ranging from beatings, having their heads shaved to being publicly hanged, six of them on a single day in October 1944. In 2005 the German government changed their status from criminal to resistance fighters and they have been recognized by Israel as 'righteous among the nations'.

!!

The Enigma of Enigma

Although little known in his own lifetime, Alan Turing is now a well-respected and admired hero of the war. There is much to say on Turing, but essentially he was a British scientist and mathematician who joined the British government's code-breaking department in 1938. His genius helped to finally crack the seemingly unbreakable 'enigma code' used by the Germans to communicate encrypted messages. The cracking of this code saved countless lives and was a great boost to the Allied war effort. Turing's work also included electronics and he is considered to be the father of modern computing. For his crucial role in the war effort, he was given a knighthood by King George VI though his classified work remained secret. Turing was only one of several boffins working at the top secret government department at Bletchley Park, but his eccentricities earned him the nickname 'prof'. He wore a gas mask to ward off hay fever (from which he suffered in the first week of every June) and chained his favourite tea-mug to railings to prevent it from being stolen. He was also a superb long distance runner and sometimes ran the forty miles from Bletchley to London for a top secret meeting.

And what happened to this man who served King and Country so diligently? Turing was homosexual and in 1952 his house was burgled. During the course of the investigation it became clear the perpetrator was a former lover and both men were tried for 'gross indecency' as homosexuality was a criminal act. Turing was given a choice of prison or probation, on the condition he accepted injections to reduce his libido. Turing chose the latter. These injections would render him impotent and his conviction meant he lost his security clearance and barred him from working with the British government's intelligence agency, which was his passion. Turing took his own life in 1954 and was 'pardoned' under the queen's prerogative of mercy in 2013.

!!

Escape Playing Cards

An ingenious plan was dreamed up by the United States Playing Card Company working with the Operation of Strategic Services and British Intelligence. They made 'map decks'. When the conventional-looking playing cards were soaked in water, the layers could be peeled apart to reveal useful maps from prisoner of war camps across Europe. They were top secret and there is no record of exactly how they were made.

It is believed that only two decks still survive; one in private hands and the other in the International Spy Museum in Washington DC.

Cards providing a totally different kind of escape were also available in wartime. In the first weeks of the war, when the Blitz was expected in Britain but had yet to happen, Black Out playing cards were all the rage. The variety of designs included a silhouette of an Air Raid Precaution warden (silhouettes of aircraft were used to familiarise the public with them) and 'A Black Out View of Piccadilly' – a black square.

!

The Eternal Jew

The Eternal Jew is one of the most despicable monstrosities to come out of the Nazi propaganda machine based on a book of 265 photographs supposedly showing Jewish antisocial types and behaviour. The 1940 movie was the brainchild of Goebbels as Minister of Propaganda and Enlightenment and was intended to stir up feelings of disgust and hatred towards Jews. Cinema was as old as the century and it was powerful and popular; for many it was the only gateway for ordinary people to life outside their own environment. Previously, there had been movies which were sympathetic to the Jews and it is likely Goebbels insisted on countering this. A 1936 British film of the same name shows the unjustified oppression of Jewish people. The Nazi version was directed by Fritz Hippler, Goebbels' head of film in the Ministry, who would try to distance himself from it when confronted by the Allies after the war. He claimed the film had no connection with the Holocaust. The screenplay was by Eberhard Taubert, an anti-Semitic lawyer known as *Anti* in Nazi circles.

The title itself comes from the medieval tale of 'The Wandering Jew'. In this, a Jew is cursed with immortality and forced to walk the earth until the second coming of Christ.

This bizarre movie is stomach churning to a modern audience and an unforgiveable manipulation of the truth. Essentially, the viewer sees a montage of real life footage from ghettoes. Over this the narrator, actor Harry Giese – acting as though it was an animal documentary – violently and insistently condemns the lifestyles of the Jews, comparing them to an epidemic disease or rats that must be annihilated. The filmmakers deliberately filmed the most destitute people or those with physical deformities. Their ill looks, torn clothes and desperate situation are portrayed as proof of the filth of Jewish culture. The fact that these people are in this state because the Nazis took them from their homes, ruined their careers and put them in the ghetto in the first place seems completely lost!

The messages of the film are also contradictory and confusing; on one hand the subjects are poor, work-shy and lazy – and on the other they are mansion-dwelling tycoons in charge of the world's economy, sipping champagne in the 'decadence' of Berlin in the days of the Weimar Republic.

Another infuriating concept of the film is the idea of Jewish people 'mimicking' and 'assimilating' with their 'hosts'. The narrator laments that many Jews are so Germanised they are almost impossible to tell from other people; unlike their ghetto kin who show their true nature. This is a ludicrous catch 22; on one hand they are demonized for staying isolated and not taking part in German culture and on the other they are attacked for not being loyal to their own roots and making an effort to integrate with their 'host' country. *The Eternal Jew* can only be shown in Germany today in specified educational establishments and under strict rules.

!

Executive Order 9066

After the Japanese attack on Pearl Harbor in December 1941, the American government had decisions to make. By definition, the United States was a vast polyglot society. There were Jews in America and there were Germans, Frenchmen, Englishmen, descendants of every European and most world races, including the Japanese. Executive Order 9066 declared that all Japanese-Americans were to be relocated from the West Coast in case they were on the side of the enemy. Despite the fact over 60% were American citizens, in total around 127,000 people were forced from their homes and made to live in one of ten internment camps. The Land of Liberty's hope was to combat the 'yellow peril' and the fears of collaboration and sabotage.

Outraged, 5,000 of those interned renounced their citizenship – though this was declared void by a federal judge. The camps themselves were similar to those in Britain that housed 'aliens' rounded up in 1939-40 by Defence Regulation 18B – anyone of German, Austrian or Italian descent. They included fairgrounds and racetracks, holding up to 18,000 inmates. All education and welfare was provided by the US government. The camps remained open until 1946 even though Order 9066 was suspended in December 1944. A 1948 law compensated those interned for financial loss and a 1998 act of Congress awarded payments of $20,000 each to the 73,000 survivors as compensation for the violation of their liberties. The legality and morality of Executive Order 9066 is still debated to this day and the anniversary of the signing of the Order is commemorated by Japanese Americans as a Day of Remembrance.

!!!
Explosive Rats

Explosive rats was the idea of Britain's Special Operations Executive (SOE). This often eccentric organization – 'Winston's wizards' they were sometimes called – was set up by Churchill himself to 'set Europe ablaze'. SO1 were the daredevil agents who parachuted behind enemy lines, linking with local Resistance groups and causing chaos with sabotage and as much disruption as possible. SO2 were the boffins, working out of Bush House in London and Woburn Abbey in Bedfordshire, to devise ingenious 'black propaganda' to cause maximum confusion and doubt in the Third Reich. Dead rats would be filled with plastic explosives and then placed near boiler rooms. The SOE assumed the Germans would throw the rats into the boilers to get rid of them and thereby cause an explosion.

The rats never saw action, being discovered by the Germans before they could be used. The Nazis were so panicked by the idea that any rat could be a bomb that they showed them to military experts and organized searches. This time wasting of military effort meant that the SOE considered it a success.

The source of the dead rats came from a London supplier, who was led to believe they were being used for University experiments.

!
The Faith and Beauty Society

The place of women in Hitler's Reich was, for most people, seen as a retrograde step. From 1933, women in medicine, the law, the media and the professions generally were expected to step down in favour of men. Anti-Nazi propaganda posters showed downtrodden frauleins kneeling before black-uniformed SS men, lovingly lacing up their boots! A woman's role was to bear the children who would carry on the Reich into the future. Mothers were given bronze, silver and gold awards for child bearing. Part of this concept was the notion of perfect Aryan womanhood – the beautiful, blonde-haired, blue-eyed Valkyrie of German Teutonic mythology.

In 1938, the Germans created the Faith and Beauty Society. This voluntary organisation was the bridge between the League of German Maidens and womanhood. The Society was open to girls aged seventeen to twenty-one in preparation for their future lives as perfect mothers. Activities ranged from home economics such as cooking and sewing, to sports, dancing and gymnastics. The girls also volunteered in the community, helping mothers raise their children and supporting the troops. Around 400,000 people took part.

The idea backfired slightly because of the overt sexuality of these girls. Just before the Society was founded, in the 1936 Nuremberg Rally, nearly 900 girls of the League of Maidens were maidens no more!

!
Fanta

Coca-Cola was originally a medicinal pick-me-up invented in America in the nineteenth century by John Pemberton and marketed by Asa Candler. Its exact composition is a closely-guarded secret, but it contained caffeine, kola nuts and coca leaves. The one billionth gallon of Coca-Cola syrup was made by the company in July 1944.

Coca Cola had a factory in Germany run by Max Keith but syrup from the United States, hostile to the Third Reich and setting up a trade embargo in 1940, became difficult to source. To keep the factories in operation, Coca Cola had a meeting to discuss a new name, with 'Fanta', the German for imagination, being the winner.

This new drink was made from a slapdash assortment of by-products and ingredients – Keith called them ‘leftovers of leftovers’ – that were available to Germany and was described as 'a light-coloured beverage that resembles ginger ale' it was actually whey and apple pomace The popularity of Fanta is unclear, but it was often used to flavour food when other flavourings were a luxury and a recipe for *Fantakuchen*, Fanta cake, is still popular.

It is perhaps unfair and incorrect to call Fanta a Nazi drink, though it did develop as a result of and in response to wartime activities. Fanta was discontinued after the war but was relaunched in 1955 and is now one of the world's most popular soft drinks. Either way, the updated recipe means the drink we know today would be unrecognisable to that enjoyed by the *Wehrmacht*. Except, that is, for the special 75th anniversary brew sold in Germany. Its glass bottles were of 1940s design and the contents included whey and apple pomace. An advertisement claiming to bring back the taste of the ‘good old times’ was removed for fear of causing offence!

!!!
Foo Fighters

'Where there's foo, there's fire' was a catchphrase of an American cartoon character, Smokey Stover and the term caught on for what US airmen also called 'krautballs'. The same paranoia that produced the phantom Fifth Column in Britain also produced ever more lurid notions about Nazi technology. Some of this was, of course, based on fact. Both sides in the war were trying to perfect jet technology and ever more powerful bombs; the ghastly results were the V1 and V2 'doodlebugs' that rained on Britain in 1944 and '45 and the flattening of Hiroshima and Nagaski in August 1945. It was no coincidence that the Nazi the Americans most wanted to meet at the end of the war was the rocket scientist, Werner von Braun who went on to lead the US space programme during the Cold War.

On 13 December 1944, General Eisenhower's headquarters (SHAEF) in Paris held a press conference to describe a new weapon that had been observed by American airmen. They looked like Christmas tree decorations, silver spheres that appeared either singly or in clusters. If they *were* weapons, no one could quite work out what they did. In a report in the New York *Herald Tribune* the next month, the 'balls of fire' had become red, flickered on and off and flew along the wingtips of American aircraft. In Britain the *Daily Telegraph* thought they were orange and they appeared *under* planes' wings with dull flashes of light. The differing physical characteristics should have been clue enough that the whole thing was suspect, but human nature loves nothing better than the inexplicable.

Unfortunately for anyone trying to sort fact from fiction in the world of air technology, on 24 June 1947, civilian pilot Kenneth Arnold reported seeing 'saucer', 'disc' or 'pie-plate' craft in the sky as he flew over Oregon's Cascade Mountains. The flying saucer legend was born and a world made hysterical by the atomic threat of the Cold War became gripped by UFOmania. That meant that test pilot Randolph Schriever's claim in 1952 that the Luftwaffe had developed these crafts as early as 1941 must be called into serious doubt. So must some of the claims made by Rudolf Lusar in a book on Germany's secret weapons, published in 1957.

As for the Foo Fighters, what were they? It is possible that they were freak atmospheric conditions, rather like St Elmo's Fire, electricity in the air that had been witnessed by sailors for centuries. They could have been ball lightning, which some physicists contend is a genuine phenomenon. What is most likely is that they were tricks of the imagination of men exhausted by flying too many nerve-wracking missions.

!!!
Fraulein Hitler

Wouldn't it have been better if Hitler was a woman? He'd be less angry, more compassionate and easier to talk to. This was what some British spies thought. Their plan was to sneak oestrogen into his food to make him less aggressive. Poison was ruled out as it would be discovered by Hitler's food testers. Oestrogen however is tasteless and the effects would not be instant, allowing for a continuous campaign of feminising. The plan was never realised but the British claimed they were perfectly able to carry it out. We will never know, but it's amusing to think how things could have been different if Hitler found himself developing breasts, having to buy a büstenhalter and feeling a bit emotional.

All in all the idea was nonsensical. Dyed in the wool Nazi females like Ilse Koch and Irma Grese, both sadistic concentration camp guards, were every bit as vicious as their male counterparts, so feminism does not guarantee niceness! Bearing in mind the Nazi opposition to women in high places (only the superb film maker Leni Riefenstahl kept her position working for Goebbels' propaganda unit) even the Fuhrer would have been removed had the oestrogen worked.

The vague background to all this is that it is just possible that Hitler was bisexual or even homosexual. His sexual appetite seems to have been small, especially in comparison with Goebbels and Goering and his relationships with women were largely platonic – his mistress Eva Braun and his niece, Geli Raubal. There were rumours that Hitler and Rudolf Hess were lovers, but actual evidence is non-existent.

As this book goes to press, an American woman, asked for her opinion as to whether the next President could be female said, 'No. What if she had hot flushes? She could start a war in ten seconds!'

!!!

Fukuryu – the Crouching Dragon

Fukuryu is Japanese for ‘crouching dragon’, but what was the word applied to? *Kamikaze* divers of course. As the Americans closed in on the Japanese Empire, the idea for these suits was to beat back any American invasion of Japan itself, which would have to come by sea. The suits allowed the wearer to breathe underwater and a 15kg mine would be placed on US ships via a 5m bamboo pole. Weighed down by their suits and 9kg of lead, the divers would walk along the seabed for hours undetected and place their mines on the hull of an enemy vessel, probably killing themselves in the process. The war ended before the Fukuryu could be widely implemented – a thousand specialised suits were ready and a further eight thousand on order – and the only deaths appear to be from suit malfunctions in training.

The divers’ suicide missions must be seen as part of the eastern mentality that produced the *kamikaze* (divine wind) airmen, who deliberately ploughed their aircraft into enemy ships. No one in other armies, even the younger fanatical elements of the Waffen SS in the war’s closing stages, accepted so resolutely that a cause was worth dying for.

!
The German Glance

Der Deutscher Blick was a glimpse of sanity in Hitler's Third Reich. The greeting 'Heil Hitler' replaced 'Guten tag' (good day) as a social convention, first with the Nazi Party and later across Germany and German-occupied territories. Originally, 'heil' meant 'salvation', as in *heiliger* (holy) and its use was required by law. It was also used in national institutions like schools and colleges, always accompanied by the extended, rigid right arm salute. Contrary to popular myth, heel-clicking was not part of this ritual; that was associated with the old Prussian officer class of the army.

The German glance preceded 'Heil Hitler' and sometimes made it unnecessary. Sceptics and opponents used it, checking right, left and behind to ensure that no one was within listening or viewing distance. Their subsequent conversations could then be carried on as normal, as though the whole country had not gone mad!

!
The Ghost Armies

The USA's 23rd Headquarters Special Troops had one objective; 'tactical deception'. Their mission was to confuse the enemy as much as possible via the art of illusion. To that end, many of its members were actors, artists and sound engineers. Their most famous work was the creation of 'ghost armies'. Over 1100 men were ordered to create vast numbers of props; inflatable tanks and rubber aircraft to give the impression of a vast concentration of forces, thereby fooling the Nazis that a particular place was to be the location of a particular attack. Over twenty of these operations were carried out, perhaps the most famous being on the English coast in preparation for D-Day.

They blasted out the sounds of moving troops into the countryside via amps which could be heard from miles away and communicated misleading Morse code and radio messages, copying the codes of real fighting units and even using the idiosyncrasies of individual radio operators.

Amusingly, they would also drive trucks around in a loop, giving the impression to any watching enemy that huge numbers of troops were being transported through the area. The unit was incredibly successful; ultimately they caused mass confusion for the enemy, convincing them that the Allies were much more powerful than they were. It is estimated their tricks saved tens of thousands of lives. The story remained classified until 1996.

!!
The Ghost Plane

On 8 December 1942, just over a year after Pearl Harbor, the US military in the Pacific detected unusual activity on their radar heading towards them. Two fighters were scrambled to investigate, but upon intercepting the plane they were confused to see it was one of their own, a Curtiss P-40 Tomahawk, but with markings that had not been used for a year. As they flew alongside the mysterious aircraft, they noticed it was riddled with bullet-holes, had no landing gear and the bloodied pilot was slumped in the cockpit. He had just enough energy to smile and wave at the interceptors, before plummeting to the ground and crashing.

At the crash site there was no sign of the pilot but they did find a diary, which suggested the plane had travelled from the island of Mindanao in the Philippines 1,300 miles away. The Americans were lost for words. Who was this mysterious pilot? How did he launch without landing gear and fly when unconscious? Where had he been for the last year? And what happened to his body?

As with most tall tales, this should be taken with a very large pinch of salt. The story of 'the Ghost Plane' is one of those urban legends where the setting, characters and theme change but the essential story remain the same. At first the story seems quite convincing, perhaps even frightening – but there is no documented source for it.

The tale actually comes from a collection of war stories told by Robert Lee Scott Jr. in *Damned to Glory*, published in 1944!

!
The Gleiwitz Incident

The Gleiwitz Incident started the war. The Nazis were ready and eager to invade Poland, but as part of their propaganda, they wanted to manipulate the truth and justify the invasion. Although Hitler expected Britain and France to do nothing to defend Poland, he wanted the world to think it was the Poles who were the initial aggressors. This was achieved on 31 August 1939. Under instructions from the Gestapo, Nazi soldiers, led by Alfred Naujocks, dressed up in Polish uniforms and attacked a German radio station called *Sender Gleiwitz*. Once inside they broadcast a provocative anti-German message.

> 'People of Poland! The time has come for war … Unite and smash down any Germans, all Germans, who oppose your war!'

To make the attack look more convincing, the Gestapo murdered a local and several prisoners from Dachau's prison camp, poisoning them with lethal injections before riddling their bodies with bullets, and dressed them up as saboteurs, leaving their bodies at the scene as 'proof' of the incident. The codename for this was the rather grisly 'Canned Goods' and the idea was dreamed up by Heinrich Himmler, head of the SS, his second-in-command Reinhard Heydrich and Heinrich Muller, the Gestapo chief.

The next day Germany would invade Poland and the Second World War would begin. Hitler referred to the incident when justifying the invasion claiming that there had been 'an attack by regular Polish troops on the Gleiwitz transmitter'. Unconcerned that it was a lie, he confided in his commanders, 'The victor will not be asked whether he told the truth.'

!
'God with Us'

The relationship between Nazi ideology and Christianity is muddled. While some leaders such as the neo-pagan Himmler were indeed atheists and wanted to abolish the church, many more believed in a 'positive' Christianity which could evolve and adapt to distance itself from the religion's Jewish parentage. Catholicism was greatly harassed by the Nazi party, with thousands of priests being arrested. While Pope Pius XI (Achille Ratti) had been protesting against Nazi excesses inside Germany since at least 1937, his successor, Pius XII (Eugenio Pacelli) has gone down in history as 'Hitler's Pope', remaining mysteriously silent over the Holocaust even though he knew what was going on.

It is probable that the Nazi leadership simply had other things to worry about than to risk discontent among the predominantly Christian German population. The Wehrmacht continued to have '*Gott Mit Uns* (God with Us)' on their belt buckles as had the German army since its creation in 1871, unlike the SS who had 'My Honour Is Loyalty' stamped on theirs.

Hitler himself seems to have had an even more confusing personal relationship with spirituality. At the age of four he was reported to have been saved from drowning by a priest. This story was known to the locals, but Hitler never spoke of it himself. It is also claimed that Hitler wanted to be a priest when he was younger. He was certainly a choirboy in his home town of Linz and the ritual of the Catholic Mass appealed to him. He mentioned God and faith in his speeches, though whether his words were what he personally believed or just for his audience is still debated.

Ultimately, it can be conjectured that hostility towards the Church was more due to the fact it detracted from loyalty and worship of the Nazi ideology. What would have happened to Christianity if Germany had won the war is unknowable and can be only the stuff of alternative history.

!!
The Gold Train

In the panic of spring 1945 as the Third Reich collapsed, there was a scramble among the Nazi high and middle command to salvage what they could of the loot taken during the war. Most of this – gold, silver, paintings, antiques – had belonged to Jewish families across occupied Europe. Rumours abounded from those months that there was an entire freight train loaded with such goodies, but mostly gold bullion bars, that vanished somewhere en route to or from the east (the stories vary).

The most persistent legend says that the train, heavily armoured against attack, disappeared inside the Owl Mountains, then in Germany, in a top secret project called Riese (giant). Over the past five years, there have been serious investigations by archaeologists and geophysicists in tunnels near the Polish town of Wlabrzych. The latest in-depth investigation – by Andreas Richter and Piotr Koper – has revealed … precisely nothing. The dig has cost $37,000 to date, a virtual money pit; but Richter and Koper refuse to give up, intending to start again in September 2016.

The legal ramifications of who exactly owns the gold – if it exists – would be horrendous, with court cases dragging on for years.

!

Goliath

Despite its name – and it's even worse in German (*Leichter Ladungstrager*) – the Goliath was tiny, standing 1ft tall and 4ft long. The tank was in fact a tracked mine, originally a French invention, but hijacked by the Germans after the Wehrmacht captured the prototype in 1940. The idea of the remote controlled gadget was to send it to attack tanks, destroy bridges and carry out general demolition. They were designed to be expendable, blowing up with their targets. They were even used in the defence of D-Day but repeated shelling cut their command cables. The weapons weren't particularly successful, having a top speed of just 6 miles per hour and hindered by their attached cables, they were also prone to getting stuck easily. American GIs often found the captured or abandoned goliaths amusing, posing with them for pictures. There are a number of them in various military museums around the world.

!
The Gran Sasso Raid

If there was any moment of the war meant for Hollywood, it was the daring Gran Sasso Raid under Operation Eiche (Oak). The only problem was, it was the Germans who carried it out. In July 1943, after the invasion of Sicily and the bombing of Rome, the Italians deposed the dictator Benito Mussolini and the king, Victor Emmanuel III, had the former Il Duce arrested and moved throughout the country. Unknown to his captors, the Germans, led by SS Captain Otto Skorzeny, were keeping an eye on things. The SS cracked a coded message to discover that their ally was being held at the guarded and fortified Campo Imperatore Hotel, deep within the Appenine mountains, high on a bleak ridge. On 12 September, around 100 SS and Paratroopers launched a daring glider raid to rescue him. They landed on the mountain and overwhelmed 200 guards of the Carabinieri without a shot being fired. A relieved Mussolini was told, 'The Fuhrer has sent me to set you free', to which he replied, 'I knew my friend would not forsake me.' He was then flown from the mountain base to a military airport, and from there to Vienna where he received a hero's welcome at the Hotel Imperial.

It was a late triumph for the Germans, though Mussolini was ruler now only in name, as the header of the Reich's puppet government, the Italian Social Republic. Skorzeny came to be regarded as the 'most dangerous man in Europe' and even Churchill was impressed by the raid.

The escapade ultimately did Mussolini no good. Trying to escape in a private's overcoat in the last days of the war, he was arrested by Italian patriots who shot him and his mistress, Clara Petacci, at an Esso petrol station in the Piazzale Loreto in Milan.

The Campo Imperatore Hotel claims that the room in which Mussolini stayed has been untouched since the Gran Sasso Raid itself.

The Great Dictator

Charlie Chaplin's 1940 movie *The Great Dictator*, remains one of the world's most influential works of cinema. The brave film is a famous parody of Hitler and fascism and was made at a time when America was still neutral. There seem to be two theories as to Chaplin's inspiration. The first is that he discovered that Hitler had placed him on his 'kill-list' for being a 'disgusting Jew acrobat'; even though, ironically, he admired the man's talent. The Nazis believed Chaplin to be Jewish as he never denied it. He was in fact English, born in the hardship of working class London.

The second theory is that Chaplin was shown a copy of the Nazi movie, *Triumph of the Will*, Leni Riefenstahl's masterpiece, a ground-breaking piece of chest puffing, showing the full might of the Reich through rallies and marches at Nuremberg. A friend of Chaplin's was so overwhelmed by the movie he said the American people must never be allowed to see it or they would lose their resolve. Chaplin found it pompous and hilarious and wanted to mock it.

The Great Dictator follows Chaplin as two doppelganger characters, a persecuted Jewish barber and a megalomaniac ruler (Adenoid Hynkel). The film is funny and poignant and a famous hope-filled speech where the barber pretends to be the dictator in front of a crowd at the end and has had a change of heart, is still moving and surprisingly relevant to a modern audience.

Famous for his silent movies, this was Chaplin's first 'talkie' and was both a commercial and critical success one of the greatest movies of all time. Hitler saw it, his responses ranging from bursting out in tears to finding it funny, depending on the source.

The film, banned, in all Nazi-occupied countries, remained unavailable in Germany until 1958. A copy was said to have been smuggled into the Balkans where a Wehrmacht audience either left the cinema in disgust or fired bullets at the screen.

!!
The Great Panjandrum

The Great Panjandrum was a British creation designed to break through the Nazi defences in Normandy. Essentially, it was two ten foot wheels joined by an axle, the wheels lined with seventy rockets and the centre filled with explosives. As the rockets were lit, the plan was for the Panjadrum to propel itself along the beach at speed, looking like a huge Catherine Wheel, roll into the German fortifications and create a giant explosion, allowing tanks to pass through.

It was the brainchild of the Department of Miscellaneous Weapons Development, also known as the 'wheezers and dodgers.'

The weapon was taken to Westward Ho! in Devon, but the experiment didn't quite go to plan. The Panjadrum flew out of control, almost knocking down the cameraman and a group of VIPs and ended with observing soldiers and civilians running for their lives. At least an excited dog enjoyed the event, chasing after a stray rocket. Fortunately the testers had changed the explosives with sand for this experiment, much to the relief of the people of Westward Ho!. Needless to say, it was never used in action.

Something very like it featured in a *Dad's Army* episode on television, but the device used there was operated by remote control radio.

The phrase was first used in an 1820 novel by Maria Edgeworth and came to mean a pompous, self-opinionated expert.

!

'Gung Ho!'

One of the most iconic photographs of the war is the picture of six soldiers raising the US flag on Mount Suribachi after the battle of Iwo Jima. The Pulitzer Prize winning picture had such an impact it was immortalised into a statue at the Marine Corps War Memorial in Arlington, Virginia, unveiled in November 1954.

It has been claimed the picture was staged, but as with most things, the truth is more complicated than that. Joe Rosenthal was the Associated Press combat photographer. He died at the age of 94 in 2006 and was always annoyed by the allegation. In an interview, his colleague Hal Buell explained how it came about. There was an earlier photograph taken by a Marine photographer, Sgt. Lowery, but his equipment was damaged during a firefight. Afterwards, the soldiers were ordered to replace the flag as it was too small and erect a larger one. Rosenthal was on site to witness this, and as the first flag was being lowered the second flag was being raised. With seconds to decide he chose to capture the latter. Sgt. Lowery's picture was fine, but didn't capture the imagination of its viewers in the same way as Rosenthal's.

Rosenthal did stage a photo, asking a group of celebrating Marines to stand around the flag in what is now known as the 'Gung-Ho!' picture. The film was sent to Guam to be developed and soon after to the American newspapers. The flag-raising picture was so impressive some thought it was staged. When Rosenthal was asked if it was, he replied 'Yes', believing they were referring to the Gung-Ho! version. Immediately, he realised the confusion and corrected his answer for the journalists. Hal Buell said it was too late 'the correction never catches up with the error. Joe spent the rest of his life defending what was alleged as a phony picture.'

The whole story formed the plot of *Flags of Our Fathers* directed by Clint Eastwood in 2006.

!!
Hermann's a German

Hermann Goering is best known as one of the Nazi high command and head of the *Luftwaffe*, but he was something of a diva too. A fighter pilot in the First World War and recipient of the coveted 'Blue Max' medal for bravery, Goering joined the infant Nazi party in Munich in 1923 and quickly became indispensable to Hitler, responsible for the Four Year Plan, part of Germany's economic revival in the late 1930s. He was fond of elaborating and personalizing his uniforms to make them as fabulous as possible. He was also obsessed with rewarding himself with medals. This amused Hitler so much that he was known to make jokes about Hermann, awarding the man medals from gold and silver paper to wear with his pyjamas.

Official records show that during the First World War, before there was a Nazi Party, Goering received eleven awards and three during the Weimar years when the Nazi Party was growing. During the twelve and a half years of the Reich, he awarded himself no less than twenty-eight decorations and gleefully accepted a further thirty-two from Germany's allies or occupied countries. Contemptuous opponents of the Nazis ridiculed such over-dressing with the term *gold fasanen* (golden pheasant).

According to Rochus Misch, who was a telephone operator in Hitler's bunker under the streets of Berlin, one of his favourite jokes went as follows. 'One day, Mrs. Goering came into the bedchamber and found her husband waving his Field Marshal's baton over his underwear. "Hermann, darling, what are you doing?" she enquired. "I am promoting my underpants to overpants!"'

!
High as Kites

A modern mind may think that a soldier in the Second World War had to be on drugs to do what they did, and there is every chance they were. The *Wehrmacht*, issued millions of tablets to their soldiers, one of the most common being the appropriately named pervitin. This was actually methamphetamine, often known today as crystal meth. Over thirty-five million tablets were issued in a four-month period alone. The Nazis were happy to hand out drugs including alcohol and opiates, on the condition that their military objectives were met.

A book published in 2015 – *Der Totale Rausch* (Total Rush) revealed that the drug was first issued in 1937 to combat stress and fatigue. Field Marshal Erwin Rommel – the Desert Fox – was believed to have been a daily user.

The Germans noted that soldiers on methamphetamine were more alert, confident and daring and were not affected by pain, hunger, thirst or sleep deprivation as much as their sober counterparts. As the war was turning, the Nazis were working on a pill to turn their soldiers into super-humans and to 'boost their self-esteem.'

Alcohol abuse was also rife, with fighting, insubordination and 'unnatural sexual acts' resulting from the excesses of the men. It wasn't just the fighting men who caved in to addiction; by the end of the war four times as many doctors were addicted to morphine than at the start of it.

Ironically, recreational drugs in Germany before the war were regarded as a Jewish perversion, but Pervertin became a rival to Coca-Cola, the American drink and was available in chocolates for civilians.

!!
Hitler the Hypnotist

During the Munich crisis of 1938, Duff Cooper, First Lord of the Admiralty, wrote that Hitler had 'cast a spell' over Neville Chamberlain, the British Prime Minister. 'I was completely horrified,' Alexander Cadogan, Permanent Secretary at the Foreign Office said, '… more horrified still to find that Hitler has evidently hypnotised [Chamberlain] to a point.' Neither man was impressed by Hitler's intellect nor his oratory; there had to be something all the more weird about the influence he was able to exert over people.

Several people referred to the famous Hitler stare. He had a habit – or was it a conscious psychological ploy? – of looking into someone's eyes for far longer than was usual. It cowed politicians, soldiers, journalists, friends and enemies and gave the impression that the Fuhrer could read minds or at least knew more about a situation than anybody else.

Arguably the most weird notion in this book and the most difficult to explain, is why millions of intelligent and decent Germans, not to mention Nazi followers in other countries, fell under such delusion for as long as they did. This can have had nothing to do with Hitler's own animal magnetism in that relatively few ever met him. The answer probably lies in the mob mentality and the madness of crowds.

!!
Hitler the Poet

As well as being a soldier, painter, author and violent oppressive dictator, Adolf Hitler was also a poet. One of his poems, *The Mother* from 1923 is a tribute to his mother who died in 1907 and it's an interesting glimpse into the mind of a man who was usually consumed with hatred.

> 'When your mother has grown old
> and with her so have you,
> When that which once came easy
> has at last become a burden,
> When her loving, true eyes
> no longer see life as once they did
> When her weary feet
> no longer want to bear her as she stands,
> then reach an arm to her shoulder,
> escort her gently, with happiness and passion
> The hour will come, when you, crying,
> must take her on her final walk.
> And if she asks you, then give her an answer
> And if she asks you again, listen!
> And if she asks you again, take in her words
> not impetuously, but gently and in peace!
> And if she cannot quite understand you,
> explain all to her gladly
> For the hour will come, the bitter hour
> when her mouth will ask for nothing more.'

There is no doubt that young Adolf was his mother's favourite. He looked like her and detested his father who he described as vicious and violent. Mothers had a special place in Nazi ideology, although, paradoxically, women did not.

!
Hitler's American

The name Henry Ford is synonymous with American enterprise and conveyor-belt mass production, making the motor car not only *the* symbol of twentieth century America but a must-have gadget bought by millions around the world. The Ford Motor Company used slave labour drawn from French prisoners of war at its German subsidiary in contravention of the Geneva Convention's Article 31 that banned such employment. Before the Americans entered the conflict, Ford supplied the Reich with military equipment, declining an offer to work with the British Royal Air Force.

He believed that all modern wars, including the Second World War, had been deliberately started by 'financier warmakers', his euphemism for the Jews. Even baseball had its problems, according to Ford – 'too much Jew'. The company produced a newspaper, *The Dearborn Independent* throughout the 1920s focussing on *The International Jew*, a series of articles written by Theodore Fritsch, a well-known anti-Semite in Weimar Germany. Heinrich Himmler was impressed by Ford – 'one of our most valuable, important and witty fighters'.

He was even praised by Hitler in his book *Mein Kampf* – 'only a single great man, Ford [who] to [the Jews'] fury still maintains full independence [from] the controlling masters of production.' The respect was mutual, both Hitler and Ford keeping photographs of the other on their office desks. In 1938 the American was awarded the Grand Cross of the German Eagle medal, which he refused to return when Germany declared war on the US.

At the Nuremberg trial of leading Nazi war criminals in 1946, the ex-Hitler Youth leader, Baldur von Shirach, claimed that Ford's *International Jew* (although he did not write it himself) turned him and many others into anti-Semites.

!!
Hitler's Jew

Eduard Bloch was a Jewish doctor from Linz, Austria, who was the Hitler family's physician, caring for Hitler's mother when she had breast cancer. Hitler was extremely grateful for this and referred to Dr Bloch as a 'noble Jew', even sending him a postcard and a picture he had painted. On his mother's death, the doctor would later recall the young Adolf was 'the saddest man I have ever seen.'

In 1939, the Nazis took over Austria in the *Anschluss* (Union) and the Reich's anti-Semitic policies kicked in. As the persecution intensified, Bloch wrote a letter to the Fuhrer. Hitler arranged his protection under the Gestapo, the only Austrian Jew to receive it. In a later biography, Bloch would say of the young child Adolf, that he remembered a modest, polite, boy with such a good mother, he could not understand how he turned out the way he did. By that time, and, again, thanks to the Fuhrer, Bloch and his family had emigrated to America.

Historians debate to what degree Bloch's part in Hitler's life had in shaping his anti-Semitism, either encouraging or discouraging it. In the memoirs that Bloch published shortly before his death from stomach cancer in June 1945, he said of the young Hitler, 'What dreams he dreamed, I do not know.'

!!
Hitler's Mischling

Ernst Hess was one of the handful of ordinary German people that Hitler personally became involved with. Although Hess was a Protestant, his mother was Jewish so he was officially a *mischling* (mixed blood). Ernst Hess had served in the First World War and had been the commander of Hitler's unit, the 16th Bavarian Reserve Infantry, known as the List Regiment.

When the Nazis first came to power, Hess was allowed to continue in the law (he had become a judge after the war) by virtue of his war record, but the Nuremberg Laws of 1935 removed all *mischling* from office by declaring them full-blooded Jews. He was forced to resign from his position in 1936 and was beaten up outside his house. Tragically his mother and sister were ordered to be removed to Theresienstadt concentration camp, wrongly believing the 'protection' also covered them. His sister, Berta, would be murdered at Auschwitz though her mother would escape to Switzerland. When Hess was summoned to appear before the SS in June 1941 he produced the letter of protection he received from Hitler. He was told it had been revoked in May and he was now 'a Jew like any other.' He would spend the remainder of the conflict as a slave labourer in Milbertshofen concentration camp near Munich.

Ernst Hess survived the war and become a successful business man. He was offered back his role as a judge but not could bring himself to work with his ex-colleagues who had been part of the Nazi legal system. He died in Frankfurt in 1983.

!

Hobart's Funnies

The disastrous Allied raid on Dieppe in August 1942 highlighted the many dangers and obstacles to coastal invasions of the mainland and it fell to General Alan Brooke, Chief of the Imperial General Staff, to find a better way. His solution was to create a new unit, the Specialized Armour Development Establishment, under Major General Percy Hobart.

Despite the implications of the nickname 'Funnies', Hobart's modified tanks were effective. They included the Duplex Drive, which was an amphibious version that could operate on land and provide cover and support to the infantry; they were used on all five beachheads of D-Day with varying degrees of success.

The 'Crab' was a converted Sherman tank fitted with metal chains which would flail the ground and clear safe passages through minefields. The 'Crocodile' was a Churchill tank fitted with a flamethrower which could reach up to 120yds, a devastating psychological weapon, particularly effective at clearing out bunkers and fortifications. Another modification which was excellent at destroying fortifications was the AVRE (Armoured Vehicle Royal Engineers). This tank was equipped with a mortar, providing speed and range that infantry mortar teams could not compete with; it fired a 40lb bomb known as a 'flying dustbin'. The 'Bobbin' was equipped with a roll of reinforced matting which it could lay out in front of itself, to create a path for vehicles which may struggle on the beach or soft terrain. There were various other tanks which could fill trenches, move troops and bridge gaps but one of the most unusual is the 'CDL' (Canal Defence Light), equipped with a strong searchlight that would be used to light up night time battles and dazzle the enemy. Altogether, fourteen different gadgets were built and used; later modifications of some of them were still in use in the Gulf War and Iraq.

!
The Honour Ring

Heinrich Himmler was obsessed with Germany's Teutonic past and one of his many quasi-medieval ideas was the SS *Ehrenring*, the Honour Ring. Nicknamed *Totenkopfring* (The Death's Head Ring) it was given to the men of the SS, a personal gift from Himmler himself. Carved with the grinning skull of Death (itself an old Prussian design) and runic symbols such as the swastika, the hagal and the sig, the ring was inscribed with Himmler's signature, the date of issue and the recipient's name. Recipients had to have three years' service, providing that their careers were 'impeccable' and the ring was to be worn on the third finger.

When an officer died, his ring was supposed to be returned to Wewelsburg Castle where it was to be stored in a sacred chest. As the tide of war turned, Himmler ordered all the Honour Rings be returned and blast-sealed into a nearby hill. By 1945, 14,500 such rings had been sent back. With the fall of Wewelsburg Castle, the rings met different fates; some were kept by their holders, others were lost and the rest were no doubt taken by Allied soldiers as souvenirs. The rings remain a sought after item by war memorabilia collectors and copies appear everywhere. As well as the Honour Ring, those who pleased Himmler could also receive Honour Swords and Honour Daggers.

The Reichsfuhrer wrote of them that they were 'a reminder at all times to be willing to risk the life of ourselves for the life of the whole'.

!!
The Horizontal Collaborators

The inhabitants of countries occupied by the Germans during the war faced a stark decision – capitulate or die. Once the French army surrendered, it was left to civilians to cope as best they could. Vichy France openly collaborated, even contributing to the roundup of dissidents like gypsies (today's Roma) to be sent to concentration camps. The free French army under Charles de Gaulle was in Britain waiting for D-Day and the chance to win back their homeland.

With the liberation of France in 1944, over 20,000 thousand distraught women were arbitrarily and publicly humiliated and attacked by mobs. They were often stripped, spat at and had their heads shaved simply for having relationships with German soldiers. After this they would then be paraded through the local town on the back of a lorry or on foot. What level of degradation the girls received was based purely on the whim of the mob. Those attacking them were often no more innocent then those they were punishing, often naïve teenage girls caught up in the excitement of the war and being seduced by German soldiers, as English girls were by the Americans. Many were prostitutes or single mothers who had no option but to work with the Germans. One woman received this treatment just for being a cleaner for the Reich. Parisian prostitutes were kicked to death for 'collaborating' with the enemy. Allied soldiers would use the same girls themselves, buying their services with food and supplies.

Stories spread that French girls, heartbroken by the loss of their *Wehrmacht* beaus, took to becoming snipers, shooting at Allied soldiers, though this was dismissed by the British high command as 'latrine rumours'.

Pictures of young French girls with their German lovers, dressing up in their boyfriends' uniforms don't invoke any anger or disgust, and it could easily happen anywhere (and did). Equally, pictures of these same crying girls being stripped and abused to the amusement of the grinning crowd doesn't sit easily as justice.

It is difficult today to understand or judge the French. Traditionally, the Germans were the enemy. As Prussians they had humiliated them in the Franco-Prussian War of 1870-71. At Versailles the French were bent on vengeance after the First World War. Yet in the 1930s, the French government was soft, guilty of appeasement and ready, it seemed, to cosy up to Hitler. After suffering years of tyranny during the occupation, attitudes of the mob are perhaps understandable. The victims had no trials, no one to speak for them, and doubtless many girls who had no part in any of it would have been caught up in the hysteria. To this day, there has never been a complete investigation into what is still, to Frenchmen, a raw subject.

!

The Horten Ho 2-29

The Horten Ho 2-29 was a prototype Nazi stealth bomber, the result of years of experimentation to find newer, more deadly technology. With its 'flying wing' design it resembles modern stealth bombers and in 1944 it must have looked bizarre as it was so far ahead of its time. Goering, as head of the Luftwaffe, had demanded much from his engineers and designers in the escalation of technology the war required. High levels of advancement were deemed essential in any future *Luftwaffe* aircraft. The plans for the Horten Ho 2-29 were put forward by the brothers Reimar and Walter Horten, and Goering approved its development.

The sleek design of the prototype flying wing meant it would be difficult to detect by enemy radar and would have been capable of bombing raids before being intercepted and could have potentially made a significant impact.

A successful test flight was made in December 1944 (a glider version was flown in the previous March) but, as with many of the Nazi super-weapons, it was too little too late. The Allies were closing in on Germany by then. There is only one surviving copy of the Horten Ho 2-29, currently undergoing complete restoration for the Smithsonian National Air and Space Museum in Washington DC and even to this day, scientists are not quite sure how technical aspects of its design were overcome in the 1940s.

!!
'Hurrah for the Blackshirts!'

The events of the Second World War, the exposure of the Holocaust and awareness of Nazi atrocities destroyed for ever the credibility of Hitler's Third Reich. Before all this, however, many people in Britain, from senior politicians to the man in the street, were impressed by Hitler's bold policies, impressed by the economic recovery of Germany and some of them shared the Nazi antipathy towards Jews. The Marquis of Tavistock, for instance, wrote at the time –

> 'We should not forget that even in our boyhood the German Jew was a byword for all that was objectionable … Indeed, there may be a bit of Hitler even in ourselves …'

Viscount Rothermere was Harold Harmsworth, a British business tycoon and owner of the *Daily Mail* newspaper; and fourteen others. He was an anti-communist and a supporter of Nazi appeasement. He admired Hitler and wanted to avoid war with the Reich, using his newspapers to spread his personal views. He was a supporter of the maverick politician Oswald Mosley who had set up the British Union of Fascists, complete with Mussolini-style black uniforms. Rothermere himself wrote a piece titled *Hurrah for the Blackshirts.*

> 'Because Fascism comes from Italy, shortsighted people in this country think they show a sturdy national spirit by deriding it. If their ancestors had been equally stupid, Britain would have no banking system, no Roman law [?] nor even any football [?] since all of these are of Italian invention.'

Ignoring the fact that Rothermere was wrong about Roman law (never a British system) and football (common to all European countries), his support for Fascism was trotted out to thousands of readers whose education was limited and who probably believed every word he wrote.

Rothermere travelled to Berlin to meet Hitler in person in 1934. MI5 papers released in 2005 show us that he wrote to Hitler several times, congratulating him on his illegal annexation of the Sudetenland and encouraging him to invade Romania in 1939. All this is at odds with the book he wrote that year, *My Fight to Rearm Britain* as the war clouds gathered. If this was a *volte face,* it was a little late – Harsmworth died in 1940, two months after the beginning of the Blitz.

!!
The Ice Ship

One of the more bizarre ideas from the British Establishment in the war was a gigantic aircraft carrier made of ice. Britain's Royal and merchant navies were being devastated by German U-boats, in the treacherous North Sea, carrying vital supplies to Soviet Russia. There was a call to see what could be done to protect ships from torpedo attacks.

An eccentric scientist, Geoffrey Pyke, rose to the challenge. He had led an extraordinary life, having been a prisoner in Germany during the First World War and had invented motor-cycle/sidecar ambulances for use in the Spanish Civil War. Pyke suggested the building of a 2000ft long aircraft carrier, made from ice and weighing 2 million tons. The project was named Habbakuk, after the Biblical prophet. Churchill was impressed by Pyke's plans and development began. Ice wasn't as impenetrable as Pyke first envisaged but an ingenious alternative was made, a mixture of sawdust and woodchips added to it in what is now known as Pykrete. This mixture was much stronger and durable than normal ice, slower to melt and easy to repair.

Testing continued and issues with melting and warping were overcome. Although the ship wouldn't be indestructible, it could be repaired in combat and it would take such a huge and sustained effort from the *Kriegsmarine* to destroy it that they would be unlikely to risk exposing their own units to counterattacks.

In the end, the plans were scuppered. The sheer amount of resources needed to construct and maintain the carrier was deemed unacceptable. The fact the ship would only manage a top speed of six knots and the construction of a suitable rudder proved difficult to overcome. Pyke remained what he had always been, a critic of the Establishment he was trying to help. One of his typically abrasive memos reads 'Chief of Naval Construction is an old woman. Signed Pyke.'

!!

The Jericho Trumpets

For anyone who has ever seen a war movie, no sound is more memorable than the famous wail of a plane hurtling to the earth, trailing black smoke before disappearing behind trees as it is shot down. Real dog fights may not have been quite so noisy. The most dreaded plane of the war was the stuka (dive bomber) or Junkers Ju 87, which was equipped with 'Jericho trumpets', propeller-driven sirens, they had no practical purpose and their usage was purely psychological. The horrible noise of these trumpets had a great effect on enemy morale and would scare and disorient those on the ground as the planes made their dive onto their target. A vital ingredient of *blitzkrieg*, the stukas' effectiveness lessened as the war progressed and there was a problem for the pilots who flew them. Such was the speed of the dive that some of them briefly passed out, occasionally with fatal results. The enemy became used to the noise so the Jericho trumpets were phased out. However, the noise was so memorable that the movies, often using real war footage in their action scenes, would frequently use stukas as the iconic terror of the skies.

!
The Kilted Killer

Tommy MacPherson was a Scottish commando with the Queen's Own Cameron Highlanders. Having been captured in the Italian campaign and having won the Military Cross, he was dropped into occupied France with a French lieutenant on 8 June 1944. Their mission was to support the French resistance and conduct sabotage and guerilla operations against the enemy. Bizarrely, MacPherson jumped into occupied territory wearing his kilt under his Denison smock. One of the local Maquis (Resistance) waiting for him was horrified and ran to his leader – 'Chef, chef, there's a French officer and he's brought his wife!'

MacPherson was a prolific saboteur and carried out many successful operations blowing up railway bridges. On one occasion he delayed a *Panzer* column heading for Normandy to repel the Allied beachhead; a three-day journey for the tanks ended up taking two weeks. His actions became so enraging to the Nazis that they placed a 300,000 franc bounty on his head, earning him the nickname 'The Kilted Killer.'

One of MacPherson's most daring actions was driving a Red Cross vehicle through enemy lines and convincing a *Wehrmacht* Major General in charge of 23,000 men to surrender. The German soldiers were pulling back and the Maquis held a vital bridge. So, with his usual plucky spirit, MacPherson pretended he had a vast army with him and had the power to order the RAF to annihilate his soldiers if the Germans didn't capitulate. The Major General agreed. MacPherson himself later commented, 'The clincher was when I told him that I was in contact with London by radio and could at any time call up the RAF to blow his people out of sight. In truth, the only thing I could whistle up was Dixie, but he had no way of knowing that.'

!

The Kindertransport

The *Kindertransport* (children's transport) programme is one of Britain's proudest moments. After *Kristallnacht* (night of broken glass) on 9-10 November 1938 the situation for German Jews was becoming dire. These two days saw 267 synagogues destroyed, 100 people killed and 30,000 sent off to concentration camps. As the eyes of the world turned to what was happening in Germany, Jewish and humanitarian agencies appealed to Britain for help. The British government agreed to take unaccompanied children and put out a BBC appeal for foster homes. The first train left for Britain on 1 December 1938, and journeys from Germany continued until 3 September 1939, the day that Britain and France declared war. The last *Kindertransport* from outside Germany came from the Netherlands on 14 May 1940, when they surrendered to the Nazis.

A number of unassuming people became heroes in this operation. Nicholas Winton, 'the Englishman of Wenceslas Square' got nearly 700 children out of Czechoslovakia. Wilfred Israel kept the British government informed of the activities following *Kristallnacht* and Rabbi Solomon Schonfeld brought 300 children from Austria.

Once in Britain, the children were looked after until they were chosen to be fostered by new families. Although more could have been done and it could never be enough, at least it was *something*. These children would probably never see their families again and most settled in Britain after the war to start new lives. In the end 10,000 children's lives were saved.

One of them wrote later, 'I have the greatest admiration for England and the English people. They were the only country that took us in. To my dying day, I will be grateful to this country.' There are statues and memorials to the children in the railway stations they used, from Friedrichstrasse in Berlin to Liverpool Street in London.

!!
Lady Death

Lyudmyla Pavlychenko was a female sniper in the Soviet Red Army and not only has one of the highest confirmed kill counts of all time, but remains the most 'successful' female sniper in history. She was born in the Ukraine just before the Russian Revolution and became a crack shot at a local rifle club while working at a munitions factory. She also obtained a degree in history from Kiev University, specialising in the seventeenth century Cossack leader, Bohdan Khmelnytsky. At the outbreak of what the Russians call the Patriotic war, she was posted to the 25th Rifle Division. Throughout the conflict she racked up 309 confirmed kills, including 36 enemy snipers and probably many more.

She was one of 2,000 female snipers and made her first kill using a Tokarev SVT-40 semi-automatic with 3.5x telescopic sight. She became a 'Nazi hunter' and would spend hours, sometimes days, watching over enemy positions from her camouflaged hideout, waiting for the perfect shot. In two and a half months, she claimed 187 kills.

Pavlychenko was wounded by a mortar in 1942 and due to her fame the Soviets used her as part of their publicity machine. She was sent on a tour of the Allied nations and was the first Soviet citizen to be welcomed by an American president. She was appalled that one American journalist commented that her uniform made her look fat and her skirt was too long. She also visited Canada and Britain, accepting donations from Coventry factory workers to pay for X-ray units for the Red Army. She paid her respects at the ruined cathedral in the city. On her return to Russia, she trained other snipers until the end of the war.

Pavlychenko would be immortalised, not only featuring on Soviet postage stamps but the focus of a song by the American folk singer Woody Guthrie during the war itself and the 2015 film, *Battle of Sevastopol.*

!!
The Last Crusade

Anyone who has seen *Indiana Jones and the Last Crusade* may be surprised to know it's not too far removed from real events. German medievalist Otto Rahn believed that the Holy Grail, the cup from which Jesus drank at the Last Supper, was not only real but has survived and was guarded by the heretical Cathars of medieval France. He became obsessed with the legends of the Grail, Parsifal and the Nibelung cycle of poems, exactly the same pseudo-history which fascinated Hitler and Heinrich Himmler, head of the SS.

Rahn's book, *Crusade Towards the Grail* came to the attention of Himmler and they met in person. Rahn became a member of the SS and was funded to continue his search. He may have soon regretted the attention, as not only was he homosexual, and punished with three months as a prison guard at Dachau but he was possibly Jewish too. 'What was I supposed to do?' he asked, along with millions of other Germans. 'Turn Himmler down?' He resigned from the SS in 1939 but Himmler was devastated by the historian's failures and gave him a choice: suicide or execution. Rahn chose suicide and was found lying, frozen to death in the Tyrol Mountains, six months before the start of the war.

!!
The Last Tojo?

Nakamura Teruo was a soldier of the Japanese Imperial Army who held out long after the war was over. He was stationed on the island of Morotai in Indonesia. When the American forces attacked he managed to survive and evade capture. The Americans moved on and continued with their 'island hopping' campaign. Nakamura remained at his post, waiting for orders, for three decades. In the time he waited, he built a shack, tamed a wild boar, took a bird for a pet and sustained himself by farming. He had been declared officially dead in 1945.

An aircraft spotted Nakamura's settlement and offered a reward for his capture. Astonishingly the locals knew about him, and he even had a friend who ran errands, but because he refused to believe the war was over, he eventually gave up and left him to it. The guide explained the Indonesians would have to dress up and act like Japanese soldiers if Nakamura was to surrender. They did, and they arrested the man on 18 December 1974. At the time of his capture, he spoke no Japanese or Chinese because he was actually from the Amis people of Taiwan, an aboriginal tribe who were considered stateless in the 1970s.

Nakamura is the last known soldier of World War Two to surrender. He returned to Taiwan to find his wife remarried and children grown up in a world he did not recognize. He died five years later.

!
The Last to Surrender?

A contender for the last to be liberated from the Reich at the end of the war is a little known small group of islands in the Channel Isles nicknamed 'The Minkies' (Minquiers in the original French). On 23 May, 1945, three weeks after the war had ended, a French fishing boat was at work off the island, and a fisherman noticed a German soldier on the beach. 'We've been forgotten by the British,' the Wehrmacht man told the boat's skipper, Lucien Marie. 'We want to surrender'.

The actual award for the very last to surrender, however, goes to the eleven men of top secret Operation Haudegen (swashbuckler), manning a meteorological station, used to determine weather patterns in Spitzbergen with its never-ending arctic summer. Due to the chaos at the end of the war, the men lost radio contact in May 1945 and were unable to get help, living off their two year supply of rations and fending off polar bears. It was not until 4 September, four months after VE Day, that a Norwegian seal hunting vessel came across them and they surrendered to the captain. The officer handed over his pistol and the captain replied, 'Can I keep this then?' Having been away from home so long, the men were in shock at the state of the nation, particularly Dresden, which had been devastated by bombings.

Spitzbergen is now used as an emergency refuge for anyone stranded.

!!
Lebensborn

For the Reich to flourish for a thousand years and for the Aryans to become the master race, they needed children, and lots of them. *Lebensborn* e.V (The Fount of Life Registered Association) was set up in December 1935 in Munich. The idea was to increase the Aryan birthrate by breeding racially pure 'specimens' irrespective of marriage or sentimental relationships.

Heinrich Himmler and various government departments believed that the only way to achieve a master-race of superhumans was by weeding out the physically and mentally weak. To this end, the notorious (and top-secret) T.4 programme was set up. The name came from its headquarters at 4, Tiergartenstrasse in Berlin. Run by Philip Bouhler and Dr Karl Brandt, it was state-orchestrated euthanasia. An estimated 50,000 people were murdered by gas or lethal injection between 1939 and 1941.

Among the Nazis policies was the banning of contraception and abortions (there were exceptions along T.4 lines) and financial incentives to mothers who had large families. Childless couples were fined. Mothers with four children would receive a bronze medal, six children would merit silver, and gold was awarded to those who had eight or more. Goebbels encouraged 'healthy eroticism' and had soft pornography produced to get the Aryans in the mood. It clearly worked for him – Magda Goebbels produced six children!

Although socially unacceptable at the time throughout the civilized world, the Nazis also quietly supported single mothers who could receive help from the SS via their *Lebensborn* project. Orphans would be raised and babies delivered in special homes, and given up for adoption if desired by the mother, providing the child was 'pure'.

The more depressing side of the desire to swell the German

population, was the kidnapping of blonde-haired and blue-eyed children from occupied eastern countries, who would be stolen from their families then be raised in Germany. This Germanization was not proved at the Nuremberg trials, but it was probably true. The children would then be given new names and 're-educated'. Children who continually complained or cried for their families too much could find themselves sent off to a concentration camp.

Roughly 16,000 children were raised in *Lebensborn* homes; in later years they would be raised in orphanages or occasionally abused by unloving foster parents. They were often unfairly stigmatized as outcasts and Nazis and many suffered psychologically as a result. Children in the occupied countries who had German fathers were also treated badly, even when the relationship was voluntary.

Post war sensationalism peddled the myth that lebensborn included coerced sex with SS men, with drugged 'Aryan' girls producing babies almost on a conveyor-belt system.

!!
The Legion of St George

The British Free Corps, also known as the Legion of St George, was the British arm of the Waffen-SS. It was the idea of John Amery, the son of a Conservative half-Jewish politician, who was Secretary of State for India.

His wife had been a prostitute but he was unable to provide her with the extravagant lifestyle she was accustomed to. They moved to France in 1936 following Amery's bankruptcy, and he spread the lie that he worked for General Franco's Intelligence Branch in the Spanish Civil War. Following the German occupation of France in 1940, Joseph Goebbels believed Amery could be a useful pawn for his propaganda and invited him to meet him in Berlin in 1942. In a similar role to 'Lord Haw-Haw' (William Joyce), Amery could become a broadcaster for the 'New British Broadcasting Station', encouraging the British to join the Nazis in their fight against communism.

Amery conceived the idea of a unit of British volunteers in the German army. He was given permission to travel the internment and POW camps and recruit 1,500 volunteers from them. His first speech was a disaster, with only one elderly academic offering to join up. By June 1943 he had recruited only 54 of his 1,500 quota, the strength never being more than 27 at any given time and some lasted only a few days. The volunteers were told they would never have to fight their countrymen and would be sent instead to fight the Red Army on the eastern front.

The lack of take up in the brigade was a disaster in the propaganda stakes. When the war finished the members of the British Free Corps were arrested, and most of the volunteers were treated reasonably mercifully. Some received jail sentences but it was generally accepted they were motivated to fight communism and not British forces. One member told MI5 that he had heard that Hitler's plan was to place Oswald Mosley as Prime Minister and

Edward VIII (by then the Duke of Windsor, governing the Bahamas) as king in the event of a Nazi victory. As for John Amery himself, he was arrested and returned to Britain to be tried for treason. He was hanged by Albert Pierrepoint on 19 December 1945 in Wandsworth Prison. The executioner would later say Amery was 'the bravest man he ever hanged' and, at least according to one account, Amery said to him, 'Mr Pierrepoint, I've always wanted to meet you, but not, of course, under these circumstances.'

The British Free Corps and its lack of success was a victory for the British, whereas other countries had volunteered into German foreign legions in their hundreds and thousands. Their impact was minimal, but the sight of SS uniforms with the Union flag on the tunic sleeves has made rich pickings for writers of alternative history ever since.

!!!
The Leningrad Symphony

Dmitri Shostakovich was a composer from St Petersburg who wrote the music for one of the world's most surreal concerts. He had been evacuated from his home town of Leningrad and wrote *The Seventh Symphony*. The piece was performed in 1941 throughout Russia, Britain and America and would eventually be performed in Leningrad itself. The Nazis and the Finns had surrounded the city of Leningrad in the Winter War and laid siege to it for a year. The appalling conditions of Leningrad in those years made it a hell on earth. Crime rocketed and the people resorted to eating pets, rats and horses; there were even 2,000 arrests for cannibalism.

But the show must go on and the conductor Karl Eliasberg was ordered to perform Shostakovich's piece. A successful musical performance was seen as an act of defiance and a psychological victory for the Soviets. The performance would require 100 musicians but due to the state of the city and its inhabitants, only fifteen from the local orchestra turned up, with many dead or too ill to perform. Rehearsals were to be six days a week but were frequently interrupted by air raid sirens and attacks and the first rehearsal only went on for fifteen minutes as the starving orchestra did not have the energy to continue. Three would die during rehearsals. The Red Army sent in their own musicians to make up the numbers.

The performance was on 9 August 1942 in Leningrad's Grand Philharmonia Hall. The Russian army even bombed the Axis besiegers on that day in the hope of not having the concert interrupted. The performance went on, with many of the orchestra shivering, starving and exhausted. Loudspeakers and radios broadcast throughout the city and to the Axis soldiers surrounding it. One audience member of the packed hall would later comment on how ill and starving everyone was, but they were still dressed in bow-ties. 'The only thing we feared was that the Germans would start bombing us. I was thinking, "God, let us listen to it to the end."'

The performance did continue to the end, and was met with ecstatic applause. Shostakovich dedicated the *Seventh Symphony* as the *Leningrad Symphony*, in respect to the bravery of the people of the city, who would have to survive another year and a half before the siege was lifted in January 1944. The siege lasted for 842 days and it is estimated 800,000 people starved or froze to death. For those who clung to life, the classical performance echoing through the streets must have been an otherworldly spectacle.

!
Lili Marlene

No self-respecting member of the Allies, whether military or civilian, during the Second World War would think of singing the *Horst Wessel* or the *War Song Against England*. Both were Nazi in origin and considered patriotic by Germans. *Lili Marlene* was different, however; it was sung by both sides. Originally called *Song of a Young Sentry*, written by Hans Leip and Norbert Schultz, it was recorded in a German studio by Lale Anderson and sold just 600 copies. It received an astonishing new lease of life however when it was one of the songs broadcast from Yugoslavia and reached the ears of Rommel's Afrika Korps. General Bernard Montgomery's Eighth Army picked it up too and both camps belted it out in the North African campaign.

Concerned about a lack of patriotism, Churchill's government got Tommy Connor (he of *The Biggest Aspidistra in the World*) to rewrite the lyrics. This version was recorded in London by seventeen-year-old Anne Shelton. Later in the war, the Anglo-German divide was neatly closed when Marlene Dietrich, a German who had fled the Nazis, made the song her own in the United States. It even became an Italian operatic number.

!!
Lord Haw-Haw

William Joyce, nicknamed Lord Haw-Haw for his posh accent, was one of the most memorable figures of the war. He was born in Brooklyn, New York, but his family returned to Ireland when he was a child. Later he lived in Britain, obtained a London university degree and applied for the Army, before eventually becoming involved in conservatism and fascism. He was attacked while stewarding a Conservative Party meeting in October 1924 by communists, leaving him with a deep scar across his face. Joyce contended that his attackers were Jews.

In 1932, he joined Oswald Mosley's British Union of Fascists, and became a popular and talented orator. He soon rose through the ranks eventually becoming Director of Propaganda and then deputy leader. Due to a difference in opinions, Mosley and Joyce fell out and he was eventually dismissed from the party. Hearing rumours that the British government intended to arrest him for his Nazi sympathies, Joyce fled to Germany with his wife in 1939, less than a month before the beginning of the war. This was the period when foreigners and anyone of dubious political affiliations could be rounded up under the paranoid government's Defence Regulation 18B and Joyce was taking no chances.

He soon found employment as a radio broadcaster with the Berlin *Rundfunkhaus* station. His English language broadcasts from the Reich became extremely popular in Britain. In a country smothered by censorship, Lord Haw-Haw's show was a rare window into the thoughts and opinion of the enemy. It may have been considered disloyal for Britons to listen to enemy propaganda but Joyce's message and his stage American-Irish-upper-class twang were so preposterous that his broadcasts were nearly as popular as Tommy Handley's *ITMA* comedy show.

Joyce continued his broadcasts throughout the war, receiving the War Merit Cross from Hitler. As the tide turned and defeat was imminent for the Nazis, Joyce can clearly be heard becoming agitated and distressed, frustrated with Britain for its 'war-mongering' and its blindness to the threat of the Soviet Union.

In the final days of the war, Joyce gave his final rambling, drunken and sometimes incomprehensible broadcast from Hamburg, a last desperate appeal from a man whose world was crumbling around him.

He was captured by the British at Flensburg near the Danish border and accidentally shot, perhaps appropriately, in the backside! He was tried for treason at the Old Bailey, despite the fact he was not a British citizen and was found guilty. His appeal was overturned. Joyce remained unwavering in his views until the end. He was hanged by the executioner Albert Pierrepoint on 3 January 1946 and is the last person to be executed for treason in Britain.

But Joyce was not the only traitorous broadcaster. American-born Mildred Gillars became 'Axis Sally', having moved to Germany in the 1920s. She told American GIs to 'go home and forget the war'. Arrested by the Allies in 1945, she served twelve years in a federal prison.

Less pernicious, perhaps, was Tokyo Rose, broadcasting to the GIs from 1943. She was probably Iva Toguri, an American citizen with Japanese parents. Convicted of treason after the war, she served eleven years in prison and was granted a pardon by President Gerald Ford in 1977.

!!
'Mad Jack' Churchill

John Malcolm Thorpe Fleming Churchill was one of the most colourful and eccentric characters to emerge from the war. His nickname 'Mad Jack' was well earned. He graduated from the Royal Military College in Sandhurst in 1926 and served with the Manchester Regiment in Burma. After leaving the army ten years later, he worked as a newspaper editor; male model; actor and bagpiper in Raoul Walsh's *The Thief of Bagdad* and represented Britain in the World Archery Championships in Oslo in 1939.

With the outbreak of the war Churchill reenlisted and joined the British Expeditionary Force in France. His unit ambushed a German patrol near L'Épinette in the Pas de Calais, with Churchill using a bow and arrow to kill a soldier, the only known death by arrow in the entire war and the most recent confirmed archer kill in combat. Churchill insisted on carrying a broadsword and believed that any officer without one was 'improperly dressed', (this despite the fact that no English regiment *ever* carried a broadsword which was reserved for Scottish regiments).

After the evacuation of Dunkirk, Churchill signed up for the commandos in June 1940, a new unit developed by Winston Churchill (no known relation) to carry out raids against the Reich. During an amphibious assault on a German garrison in Vågsøy, Norway, Churchill, still a keen piper, began a solo performance of 'March of the Cameron Men' inside the first landing craft to disembark. Whilst in Italy, he took 42 Germans prisoner with an NCO and his broadsword. A raid that did not go to plan, due to the hesitancy of supporting partisans in Yugoslavia, saw the survivors of Churchill's unit all killed by mortar fire except him. He played on his bagpipes while waiting for his own death, which didn't come. As he was playing 'Will Ye No Come Back Again?', he was knocked unconscious by a nearby explosion. As a commando he should have been executed. Hitler's decree of 18 October 1942 ran;

> 'From now on, all enemies on so-called commando missions in Europe or Africa, challenged by German troops … whether armed or unarmed, in battle or in flight, are to be slaughtered to the last man.'

The Wehrmacht captain who captured Churchill had either never read that or he was not prepared to follow that order. He refused to hand him over to the SS. 'You are a soldier, as I am. I refuse to allow these civilian butchers to deal with you.'

In September 1944 as the Allies pushed the Germans back across France, Churchill was captured and sent to Sachsenhausen, Berlin's own concentration camp. He escaped but was recaptured near Rostock. As the war came to a close, the SS guards abandoned the prisoners and Churchill walked 90 miles to Verona, where he met up with an American patrol. The close of the war was sad news for a man like Churchill, who commented 'If it wasn't for those damn Yanks, we could have kept the war going another ten years'.

!

The Madonna of Stalingrad

The Siege of Stalingrad, fought between August 1942 and February 1943, was a hellish battle of unbelievable proportions that would claim more soldiers' lives than the entire Western front. An estimated 1.7 million men were killed, wounded or captured. This battle was the eye of the storm and the German defeat there would mark the beginning of the end of the Reich.

Leutnant Kurt Reuber was a doctor in the *Wehrmacht*, stationed near the front lines of the battle to receive the wounded and dying. He was a talented artist and a Protestant pastor before the war. To cheer up the soldiers, he drew a sketch that would become known as 'the Stalingrad Madonna', a maternal image of Jesus being cradled by Mary. All who entered the trench where he worked would see it, and some – coming from any number of unimaginable horrors – would break down in tears at the sight of it. The dug-out was too cramped to work properly and he had to stand on a stool to look down on the charcoal work as he drew it.

In a letter home, Reuber explained that the image was meant to represent 'security' and 'mother love' for those who saw it and contained the text, 'light, life and love.'

A Christmas day celebration among the medical staff and the sick was cut short by nearby explosions, killing many in attendance. The charcoal Madonna was flown out by Dr William Grosse, Reuber's commanding officer, in the last plane to leave the area before General von Paulus' Sixth Army surrendered to the Soviets. Reuber was captured and died in a Russian POW camp in 1944; his letters and his pictures were returned to his family.

The Stalingrad Madonna remains a powerful image; that such a piece of art could be created in the hell on earth of Stalingrad did much to reconcile foes after the war. The picture now hangs proudly in the Kaiser Wilhelm Memorial Church in Berlin. Copies are also on display in cathedrals in Coventry and Volgograd.

!

The Magician Who Won the War

Jasper Maskelyne was a British stage magician, whose grandfather had been the most famous illusionist on the Victorian stage. With the outbreak of war, Maskelyne joined the Royal Engineers where he convinced his superiors to let him put his skills to use. One account suggests he impressed officers by creating the illusion of a German warship in the Thames using mirrors and a model. He was transferred to the Camouflage Development and Training Centre at Farnham Castle in 1940 but found it dull. He entertained his comrades every evening but, as one remembered, was 'rather unsuccessful' at disguising 'concrete pill-boxes' which was what he was really there for. He went on to work with the secret service department MI9 in Cairo. However, by 1942 the British command appeared unimpressed, and Maskelyne was now being used as entertainment for the troops with magic and card tricks.

Opinion on his contribution to the war is divided. Some claim he created entire armies in the desert and could hide the Suez Canal. Others point out there is no record of this and the magician was more interested in tall tales and creating his own legend. He did design gadgets for captured POWs, such as a comb that could turn into a knife and a compass inside a jacket button. Maskelyne's tragedy (he died a bitter drunk in 1973) is that he spent so much time telling everybody how spectacular his 'magic' was that he probably came to believe it.

!

The Man Who Nearly Shot Hitler

Henry Tandey was the most highly decorated British soldier of the First World War, receiving the Victoria Cross, the Distinguished Conduct Medal and the Military Medal and was mentioned five times in Despatches. A career soldier, he joined the Green Howards Regiment in 1910, fighting at the First Ypres, the Somme and Passchendaele. He is also remembered for one apparent moment that, if true, could have changed the course of history.

On 28 September 1918, the British took the village of Marcoing from the Germans. As the firefight raged, it is alleged that an injured German soldier entered Tandey's line of sight but he took pity on him and did not fire, saying, 'I took aim but couldn't shoot a wounded man. So I let him go.'

In 1938, during the failing peace talks between Britain and Germany over the Munich crisis, the Prime Minister, Neville Chamberlain, met Hitler in Bavaria. A photograph of Tandey carrying a wounded comrade emerged in the British newspapers, and was then painted by an Italian artist named Fortunino Matania. A copy of that picture, *Painting of Menin Crossroads*, was in Hitler's possession. 'That man came so near to killing me that I thought I should never see Germany again,' the Fuhrer explained to Chamberlain. He then asked to have his best wishes and gratitude passed on to the man who spared his life.

The truth of this story is difficult to separate from the legend and official records are not supportive. However, it *is* known that Hitler personally requested a copy of Matania's painting in 1937. Henry Tandey never denied the incident either and believed it to be true. In 1940, as Britain was on the run from Germany and defeat seemed imminent, Tandey, by then back in his native Leamington, said he regretted sparing him, 'If only I had known what he would turn out to be. When I saw all the people, woman and children he had killed and wounded I was sorry to God I let him go.'

!!

The Man Who Never Was

Operation Barclay was the codename for a deception. The Allies had to convince the German High Command that their objective, early in 1943, was the invasion of Sardinia. In fact, it was Sicily. To pull this off, Operation Mincemeat was developed as an offshoot of Barclay and was the brainchild of Charles Cholmondeley of the RAF and Ewen Montague of the Royal Naval Reserve. The idea, like something out of a spy novel, was to dump a body at sea so that it would be washed up on the coast of neutral Spain and the papers it was carrying (false information re the invasion) would find their way into German hands.

The whole thing seemed unbelievable. In fact, younger cinema-goers, seeing the movie version in 1956, assumed that it was fiction. The biggest problem was finding a suitable corpse. With the help of the legendary forensic scientist Bernard Spilsbury and an obliging coroner, Bentley Purchase, a suicide was found that fitted the bill. Mentally ill Glyndwr Michael had killed himself with rat poison. The chemical reaction that resulted made it appear that the death was caused by pneumonia. Michael, who had no known relatives, became Acting Major William Martin of the Royal Marines. He was even given a girlfriend, 'Pam', who was actually Nancy Leslie, a typist with MI5. Her photo and love letters were found in the dead man's wallet when he was washed up from a fictitious plane crash on 30 April in Huelva, where he was buried with full military honours on 2 May.

Messages intercepted from the Ultra codebreakers at Bletchley Park proved that the Germans had fallen for Mincemeat hook, line and sinker and directed troops in the wrong direction as a result. On 9 July, the Allies invaded Sicily and it took three days for any serious opposition to arrive. 'Operation Mincemeat' was perhaps the most successful deception of the entire war and saved thousands of Allied lives.

!
The Man Who Survived

Tsutomu Yamaguchi is the only person acknowledged by the Japanese government to have survived the nightmare of the atomic blasts of both Hiroshima *and* Nagasaki. By the summer of 1945, the American president, Harry S. Truman, made the fateful decision to force a Japanese surrender quickly by using the atomic bomb that American scientists under Robert Oppenheimer had been working on. Having worked for Mitsubishi Heavy Industries for years, Yamaguchi was in Hiroshima on a three-month assignment. It was 8.15am on 6 August 1945 and he had just doubled back for the railway pass he had forgotten. The B-29 Superfortress *Enola Gay* flew overhead and dropped its deadly bombload three kilometres away. This was 'Little Boy' and its blast instantly killed around 80,000 people. Yamaguchi was left burned, temporarily blinded and deaf in one ear.

The next day Yamaguchi left the devastated city to return home to Nagasaki where he was reunited with his family. As he was explaining what had happened to Hiroshima to the company director on 9 August, a second bomb, 'Fat Man' was dropped at 11am from the B-29 *Bockscar*, bringing carnage yet again and ending tens of thousands of lives including radiation poisoning that began to spread among Allied POWs, and Korean forced labourers as well as Japanese in the town. This time, Yamaguchi was unhurt, but had a fever for a week. He became a campaigner for the abolition of atomic weapons and died in 2010 at the age of ninety-three.

!
Max Heiliger

Max Heiliger didn't exist. He was a fictional character invented by Walter Funk, president of the Reichsbank and Himmler's SS as a front for the possessions stolen from victims of Nazi genocide. The name was a cynical and supposedly humorous play on the German word for Saint and was the code of the SS bank accounts used to launder anything from wedding rings, cash and gold fillings from the dead and imprisoned during the Holocaust. The items were also referred to as 'the property of resettled Jews' and filled several Berlin bank vaults by the end of 1942. The valuables and possessions of these 'resettled' people were then sold in pawn shops or melted down into gold bars. This internal embezzlement scheme helped self-fund the Holocaust.

Funk himself was found guilty on three counts at the Nuremberg trials and was sentenced to life imprisonment at Spandau. He was released in 1960 because of ill health.

!!
Maximilian Kolbe

As in any war, individual acts of heroism stand out among the carnage and misery, but few can match the quiet intensity of the 'saint of Auschwitz', Maximilian Kolbe. He was a Catholic priest from Poland and as a child in 1906, he was visited by a vision of the Virgin Mary. He said –

> 'That night I asked the Mother of God what was to become of me. Then she came to me holding two crowns, one white, the other red. She asked me if I was willing to accept either of these crowns. The white one meant that I should persevere in purity, and the red that I should become a martyr. I said that I would accept them both.'

Kolbe would spend the rest of his life promoting the veneration of Mary.

Kolbe had a varied and interesting life with the Franciscan order, even founding a monastery in Japan which miraculously survived the atomic bomb blast on Nagasaki which struck the other side of the hill on which it was built. When Poland was occupied by the Nazis, the priest gave sanctuary to 2,000 Jews in the friary of Niepokalanów, realising perfectly well that his kindness could lead to his death. He continued to publish many written works on his views of fascism from the monastery, eventually being arrested for it and finally ending up in Auschwitz.

Kolbe's treatment there was appalling. He was often the victim of violence from the kapos, the brutal warders whose job it was to make inmates' lives a misery. When a small number of prisoners escaped, the Nazis decided to punish ten prisoners with starvation in an underground bunker as a deterrent to others. Ten men were randomly selected and one of them cried out, 'My wife! My children!' Kolbe offered to take his place.

Inside the underground bunker, Kolbe prayed for the nine souls with him. Without food and water, all of them would be dead with two weeks, except the priest. The guards were astonished to see that the man was still alive. How did they respond to this miracle, when a man shouldn't last more than three days? They gave him a lethal injection of carbolic acid. He went to the fires on 15 August 1941, the day of the assumption of the Virgin Mary.

The man that Kolbe swapped places with was a Polish army sergeant named Franciszek Gajowniczek. After the war he was reunited with his wife, though sadly his sons had already been killed by the Russians. Franciszek never forgot what the priest did for him and championed his saviour's message, saying to an American church through a translator, 'so long as he ... has breath in his lungs, he would consider it his duty to tell people about the heroic act of love by Maximilian Kolbe'. Franciszek died in 1995.

In 1982, Kolbe was declared a saint by Pope John Paul II who said he was 'the patron saint of our difficult century'.

!

Mein Kampf

What does every girl want on her wedding day? A copy of *Mein Kampf*, of course. 'My Struggle', was Hitler's famous autobiography written while in Landsberg Prison following the aborted Munich Putsch. It was considered a holy book to the most ardent Nazis. At every wedding throughout Germany, the happy couple would receive a leather bound copy of their leader's writings and every member of the armed forces had to own a copy too.

This wasn't quite as altruistic as it seems, as the local council was forced to buy their own copies using taxpayers' funds, landing Hitler a ten per cent royalty for each sale. By 1939, the book had been translated into eleven languages and sold 5.2 million copies and a special Anniversary Edition was produced, combining Volumes One and Two.

The icing on the cake was that once Hitler was in charge (becoming Chancellor in 1933), he decided he shouldn't have to pay any taxes and wrote off his own debts, including the slice of royalties that should have gone to his publisher.

Interestingly, despite the book's commercial success, Hitler seemed to regret writing it after he became chancellor. *Mein Kampf* was finally republished in Germany in 2016, the first time since the end of the war. His second book, largely on foreign policy, sank without trace, to the extent that it doesn't even have a title, being known simply as 'Hitler's second book'. Only two copies are known to exist and one of them was discovered in a German air raid shelter by an American officer. Even less readable than *Mein Kampf, der Zweites Buch* was badly translated into English in 1962 and an authoritative version as recently as 2003.

!
Molotov Cocktails

A Molotov cocktail is another name for a petrol bomb or 'poor man's grenade', a relatively simple incendiary weapon which came to popularity during the Spanish Civil War as an anti-tank device. It was widely used during the war and even issued to the British Home Guard under the auspices of General William Ironside, if only because the 'cocktails' could easily be made by civilians at home. The name itself was given by the Finns, who fought against the Soviet Union during the Winter War of 1939-40. Vyacheslav Mikhailovich Molotov was the Soviet foreign minister and announced on radio that the aerial bombardment against Finland was in fact the dropping of food and humanitarian aid to the starving population.

The humour of this was not lost on the Finns, who referred to these bombs as 'Molotov bread baskets'. From there the petrol bombs used to repel the Soviets were eventually referred to as 'Molotov cocktails'.

!!!
Mr Chad

There are a few theories as to the rise of the 'Mr Chad' graffiti. One of the most commonly accepted views is that it was conflated with the 'Kilroy was here' graffiti introduced by the American GIs and possibly used by them before America's entry into the war in December 1941. A 1946 *New York Times* article wrote 'During the war [James Kilroy] was employed at the Bethlehem Steel Company's Quincy shipyard, inspecting tanks, double bottoms and other parts of warships under construction. To satisfy superiors that he was performing his duties, Mr. Kilroy scribbled in yellow crayon "Kilroy was here" on inspected work. Soon the phrase began to appear in various unrelated places, and Mr. Kilroy believes the 14,000 shipyard workers who entered the armed services were responsible for its subsequent world-wide use.' As a humorous tribute, American servicemen then began writing 'Kilroy was here' wherever they could.

Meanwhile in Britain, another piece of graffiti was emerging. A long nosed man named Mr Chad began peering over a wall with the phrase 'Wot? No [blank]', the blank representing something the country was short of due to rationing, such as 'Wot? No Bananas?', 'Wot? No Petrol?' and 'Wot? No Spam?'. The origins of Mr Chad are not certain either, but one theory is that a lecturer discussing the effect of a capacitor in a circuit drew a diagram on a board, which looked similar to a face, with one student then writing 'Wot? No Electrons?' underneath it – as the electrons would have been discharged.

The figure may also have been invented by the Australians, perhaps as early as the First World War. There he was called Foo and appeared first on the side of railway carriages used by the Australian army.

Mr Chad and 'Kilroy was here' became fused and he started to pop up throughout the world, from British pubs and the Houses of

Parliament where someone had drawn 'Wot? No Tories?' in 1945 after Clement Atlee's Labour victory over Winston Churchill. Mr Chad followed the soldiers into battle too, appearing everywhere from Japanese pillboxes to Nazi strongholds to gents' lavatories. In the last instance, one common variant on the theme runs –

> 'Clap my hands and jump for joy'
> I was here before Kilroy.'

to which another wag added –

> 'Sorry to spoil your little joke;
> I was here, but my pencil broke.
> Kilroy.'

!!!
Mrs O'Grady

The British government was convinced, especially in the early stages of the war, that there was a Fifth Column operating in the country. A network of spies, they feared, was providing the Germans with vital information to ensure the overthrow of the last European country not to have fallen to the Nazis. This delusion can be called weird in itself but there was one piece of evidence that seemed to prove that the paranoia was not misplaced.

Dorothy O'Grady lived at Sandown in the Isle of Wight where she ran a boarding house. The island was a sensitive area that was within the defence perimeter of the naval base at Portsmouth. She spent a lot of time pestering soldiers who patrolled the barbed-wire beaches of the Island, made positive comments about Hitler and wore little swastika flags sewn into the lining of her coat. Her husband, meanwhile, was away on active service. In August 1940, she was charged with being in a prohibited area and skipped bail. Detailed maps and sketches of the coast were found in her home and in December, she was sentenced to death under the Treachery Act for sabotaging telephone wires in an attempt to impede army movements. There were rumours that she was part of a nest of British Union of Fascists centred on Southsea, but that was never proved.

What is more weird here? A British housewife acting as a saboteur for the Nazis or a British government that was planning to hang her for it? In the event, it was decided that she was clearly deranged, a mentally disturbed masochist according to the prison psychologist at Holloway, and her sentence was commuted to fourteen years in prison.

In later interviews, she claimed that the whole thing was 'a huge joke'.

!!!
Nazi Sex Dolls

The Second World War is one of the biggest hotbeds of history for rumours, hoaxes and wild claims. Although it has been widely discounted, one of Hitler's most innovative plans led to the invention of the blow up doll, which would be distributed to the Wehrmacht.

The story goes that the High Command were concerned about the rise of syphilis among the men who were frequenting brothels in Paris. Hitler approved the creation of the sex dolls to be sent to the men, which could be carried in their backpacks and inflated in time of need, to stop them visiting prostitutes. The idea was called the Borghild Project and was the brainchild of the Racial Hygeine and Demographic Biology Research Unit.

Amusingly, after thorough testing, reports suggest when the first fifty were ready to go out that soldiers refused to carry them for fear of embarrassment if they were captured by the enemy. For those who believe the tale, the bombing of Dresden wiped the sex doll factory and its evidence from the face of the earth. Experts have dismissed this story, but it has never quite gone away and some claim that the blonde, blue-eyed polymer versions were modified for children and became Barbie years later!

!
The Negro Soldier

The first African-American soldiers were recruited in North Carolina during the American Civil War and two cavalry regiments – the 9th and 10th – continued to serve the US government against the plains Indians in the 1870s and '80s. Units like this had white officers and the attitudes of many white Americans remained hostile to the idea of the free negro long after the Civil War was over.

The Negro Soldier was an American propaganda movie produced by Frank Capra for the US War Department. Capra had produced a series called *Why We Fight*, designed to encourage public favour for the war. This 1944 feature was created in the hope that more black men would sign up. While the film itself is perhaps not very offensive, the subliminal message is manipulative. *The Negro Soldier* emboldens black men to fight and die against racist Germany and promotes the positive contribution black people have made to America, showing recruits enjoying their training.

Black soldiers in the Second World War were treated harshly by their white comrades and even the uniform didn't stop abuse. The units were heavily segregated and when the GIs arrived in Britain and later France, the locals couldn't fathom why the white Americans were so hostile to the blacks. Fights often broke out between black and white army units, often over the fact that black soldiers were dancing with white girls (something that many states did not allow). It is a measure of how ludicrously politically correct we have all become that today, even the title *Negro Soldier* would cause offence to some.

!!
The Night and Fog Decree

President Franklin D Roosevelt rightly called 7 December 1941, when the Japanese attacked Pearl Harbor, 'a date that will live in infamy'. But it is infamous for another reason too. That was when Hitler decided on the *Nacht und Nebel erlass*, the Night and Fog decree, which was designed to obliterate enemies of the Reich. From that day on, anyone who was declared a dissident, in Germany or German-occupied territory, was to simply disappear. 'The prisoners,' ran the decree, 'will vanish without a trace. No information may be given as to their whereabouts or fate.'

What is weird about this is not the decree itself but that a government should give such a melodramatic name to it. It comes from Hitler's obsession with Teutonic mythology and from the *Ring* cycle of his favourite composer, Richard Wagner. 'Night and fog,' wrote Wagner, 'make you no one.'

!

No Smoking!

One of the more surprising ideas to come out of the Reich was the most advanced anti-tobacco campaign of the age. Previously, those who were anti-smoking were dismissed as the lunatic fringe or equated with the same puritan ethic that disapproved of any enjoyment. The most famous anti-smoker in history was James I, king of England, who wrote an attack on 'the noxious weed'. But then, he also believed completely in the power of witches!

In post war Germany, the infant Nazi Party had their own roll-ups, called, appropriately, Anti-Semit, but by 1939, a study from the German scientist Franz Muller revealed the link between smoking and cancer and the dangers of passive smoking. For the Nazis, hell bent on physical perfection and 'racial hygiene' this was unacceptable. Hitler went from being a heavy smoker (up to forty a day) to finding the habit decadent and the American Indian's revenge for the white man having given him hard liquor!

In 1941, the heroically named 'Struggle Against Tobacco' was formed, led by an SS officer. The Reich became pioneers in health and wellbeing, information leaflets were distributed, encouraging people to give up. Counselling and medication was offered to addicts and smoking was banned in places like schools and cinemas. It annoyed Hitler that Herman Goering, Martin Bormann (the Nazi Party leader) and his own Mistress, Eva Braun, were unrepentant smokers.

Smokers in Germany were liberated in 1945. The campaign fell apart with the end of the Nazi government and smoking levels began to rise again. The research of the Reich was either unknown or ignored by the victorious Allies and the British scientist, Richard Doll, was knighted in the 1970s for being the first to show the links between smoking and cancer.

!
The Nobel Peace Prize

Another story blown out of proportion is Hitler's nomination for the 1939 Nobel Peace Prize, a prestigious international award for champions of peace and brotherhood. Hitler *was* nominated for this prize by the Swedish politician Erik Brandt, but there is much more to it than that. Laying aside the bizarre situation that the creator of the Peace prize (actually one of the fraternity), Alfred Nobel, was the inventor of dynamite and that he was called 'the merchant of death', some very odd people have been nominated for the award and same very deserving ones have been overlooked.

At the time of the Munich Crisis (1938) the British Prime Minister, Neville Chamberlain, was nominated, but his name was quickly withdrawn when the Norwegian government pointed out that in his capitulation to Hitler, Chamberlain was 'the front runner for handing over a small country to destruction, possible annihilation'. Three days later, Brandt proposed Hitler –

> 'By his glowing love for peace, earlier documented in his famous book *Mein Kampf* – next to the Bible perhaps the best and most popular piece of literature in the world ... Adolf Hitler is by all means the authentic God-given fighter for peace and millions of people all over the world put their hopes in him as the Prince of Peace on earth.

After intense public outrage, Brandt withdrew his nomination and claimed it was an ironic joke. Historians debate whether it was in fact a joke taken out of context or as a way for him to play down the unexpected hostility he received. Brandt's actions would suggest the former, since he later protested Sweden's refusal to take more Jewish refugees and spoke out against their treatment at the hands of the Nazis. So over the top was his endorsement of Hitler that he cannot possibly have been serious. On the other hand, there were more sensible ways to demonstrate opposition to the Nobel Commission's decision-making.

An important and overlooked part of this incident is that Hitler was outraged by the prize. In 1935, the German pacifist Carl von Ossietsky was awarded it. He was languishing in a concentration camp, convicted as a traitor for his whistle-blowing and exposing German rearmament and died in 1938. Hitler was incensed that a treacherous criminal and enemy of the Fatherland could receive such a prestigious award. He forbade any German from receiving the prize and the press were banned from even mentioning it. In this context, Brandt's nomination as an irony makes perfect sense.

Either way, the Nobel Peace Prize has no control over who is nominated for the award and Hitler was never shortlisted for it.

!!
Operation Starfish

The bombing of Coventry in November 1940 was so devastating that a new word – 'coventrate' – entered the language. In a bizarre attempt to lessen the impact on real cities in the Blitz, Colonel John Turner, newly retired from the Air Ministry, came up with the idea of decoy sites, given the codename 'Q'. They had been devised as early as the outbreak of war, with the example of the Spanish city of Guernica, blitzed during the Civil War, in mind. Daytime sites – 'K' - made aircraft, aircraft hangars and entire airfields out in the countryside. The 'Q' sites proper were the night-time equivalent, with lights mounted on poles to replicate an airstrip.

By the end of 1940, the idea had extended to 'S.F.', 'Special Fire'. Decoys were set up – controlled fires in concrete pill boxes dotted around the country. In a decade when pilots relied on the visual as much as their instrument panels for finding targets, this made some sense. 'S.F.' became known as Starfish to those in the know, but it is debatable how effective the idea was. One book on the subject suggests that 968 tons of German bombs missed their real target as a result, and there were 237 Starfish sites by the end of the war. On the other hand, it meant that random bombing now took place over the countryside, putting otherwise safe villages at risk.

!!! Parachuting Nuns

They first came out of a deadly sky in May 1940. The Dutch Foreign Minister, Eelco van Kleffens, reported that parachutists had landed in Holland wearing priests' cassocks, nurses' uniforms or nuns' habits. He wrote it all down solemnly in *The Rape of the Netherlands* which appeared later that year.

Stories of nuns shaving and German troops caught putting the habits on under hedgerows and behind haystacks began to emerge from the British army pulling back to Dunkirk. Neither the otherwise paranoid Ministry of Information nor the more sensible Mass Observation Unit took these stories seriously. An MOI report from 24 May reads, 'the usual crop of rumours about "hairy-handed nuns" and parachutists', adding one about a gang of blind refugees armed with machine guns.

Harold Nicholson, Parliamentary Secretary to the MOI said in one of his brilliant radio broadcasts for the BBC, that 'Mr Chatterbug' (the epitome of loud-mouthed hysteria which could unsettle a nation) was sitting in a train when a nun in his carriage dropped her Bible. As she picked it up, Mr C. very clearly saw a muscular male wrist and the tattooed name of Adolf Hitler.

The disturbing thing about these silly rumours was that men who should have known better, like Winston Churchill, believed at least some of them. As First Lord of the Admiralty early in 1940, he accepted that there was an active Fifth Column of at least 20,000 people operating all over Britain. It may be that the government actually welcomed such rumours because it took the attention of the public away from military cock-ups, of which there were many.

!!!
Parachuting Sheep

Benito Mussolini saw himself as a latter-day emperor, commanding invincible armies and recreating the 'grandeur that was Rome'. One of the few geographical areas still available for such conquest was Africa, specifically Ethiopia, so the Italians were caught up in the unforgiving Danakil Desert, known for its oppressive heat, during the second Italo-Ethopian War from 1935-36. The area is volcanic and was described by the prestigious *National Geographic* magazine at the time as 'the cruellest place on earth'. It has been claimed that the Italian army were fussy eaters, but it's more likely the technology for pre-packaged rations had not yet been fully developed so feeding the Italian army and stopping rations from spoiling, became an issue. Either way, the army needed to move fast and be fed.

The solution to this? Planes could fly in much-needed water, but how about fresh meat? That answer, too, was simple – parachute sheep straight to the soldiers. Seventy-two sheep and two bulls did their bit for the war effort and served in Mussolini's flying column. How delicious they were or whether they survived the landing is not known. This was not, in fact, the first time that flying livestock had been seen. In the 1780s, the ballooning Montgolfier brothers tested primitive parachutes by dropping sheep from farm rooftops.

!!
Pets' War

Inevitably, in a country that set up the Royal Society for the Prevention of Cruelty to Animals as early as 1824, there was concern for family pets during the Blitz. The RSPCA recommended a hood, placed over the dog's cotton-wool-filled ears and tied under its chin to minimise the noise of explosions. Wisely, the officials warned that 'few cats will tolerate anything of the kind'. Since the cotton-wool pads were to be placed under the ear flaps and not in the ears themselves, only certain breeds would feel the benefit. German Shepherds, for example, would not be able to use these hoods!

Pet food was at a premium, just as human food was and again, the RSPCA suggested mashing up and boiling stale bread (toasted), cabbage, cauliflower, brussels sprouts and turnips. A similar stodge was recommended for caged birds.

In the meantime, some hopefuls called upon Parliament to provide a small milk ration for cats.

!!!
Pigeon Guided Missiles

Pigeons had been used for years as carriers of messages in warfare, most notably from one trench to another in the First World War, but the Second World War saw an entirely new role for them. 'Project Pigeon' was the idea of American psychologist and Harvard professor Burrhus Skinner. He believed that the accuracy of missiles could be increased by training pigeon pilots to sit in them as they were fired and guide them from within. Skinner designed a missile that had three windows to look through in the nose cone where the pigeons, in a sock to limit their movement, were placed. The 'pilots' were specially trained and conditioned to peck at the windows when they saw their target and to keep it in the centre of their vision. If the missile began to go off course the pigeons would tap the window which would alert the sensors of the missile when a window had been pecked and the tailfins would then change direction accordingly and guide the explosive and its passenger to the target of choice.

Despite the absurdity of this, the project appears to have been a great success – with the kamikaze pigeons working better than expected. The only reason for its cancellation was that the military commanders wanted to direct their resources into other projects. Skinner complained, 'no one would take us seriously'.

!!! The Riddle of Rudolf Hess

Perhaps the single most weird incident of the Second World War happened on the night of the 10/11 May 1941 when Rudolf Hess, Hitler's deputy in the Third Reich, took off from Augsburg airfield in a Messerschmitt Bf110 and crash-landed hours later at Eaglesham, Scotland. Hess himself bailed out and was captured within minutes, spending the rest of his long life in various prisons. His purpose, most researchers believe, is that he was attempting to broker a peace deal with British dissidents anxious to remove the war-mongering Churchill and bring the war to an end. The controversy rages over who exactly Hess thought he was going to meet – such people could have been hanged for treason – and whether the whole thing was an example of Hess's own delusions or whether he was lured across by British Intelligence.

Two particularly odd incidents stand out in this bizarre story. The first is that it had been predicted in fiction. In 1940, Peter Fleming, brother of Ian who would go on to create James Bond in the Cold War era, wrote a novel called *Flying Visit* in which Hitler himself parachutes into England. Was this purely coincidence or had Rudolf Hess seen a copy (his English was pretty good) and had it given him the germ of an idea?

The first that Churchill knew of Hess's arrival was when he was briefed by telephone at Ditchley Hall, his 'safe house' near Blenheim. Having been informed that an airman looking remarkably like Rudolf Hass had arrived, he went to see a private screening of a Marx Brothers comedy at the house. The obvious explanation is that Churchill already knew about the Hess flight, because it was, indeed, engineered by British Intelligence with the Prime Minister's blessing. If he did *not* know, going to watch the Marx Brothers at so crucial a time would have given both Churchill's allies and his enemies pause for thought over the man's sanity!

!!!

Round corners – Krummlauf

Much of the hand-to-hand fighting in the Second World War, by commandos as well as regular assault troops, took place in cities, towns and villages where buildings provided both cover and death-traps, depending on their situation. The obvious problem of physics is that a soldier cannot see what is hidden around a corner! One solution was a Krummlauf (bent barrel), an attachment for the Sturmgewehr 44 assault rifle used by the Germans. There were many variations from a 30 degree bend all the way up to 90 degrees. The concept of the Krummlauf was to allow soldiers to continue firing without breaking cover; a complex scope allowed them to do this. The bent rifles weren't particularly effective, having a short life span and questionable accuracy.

The Russians issued a variant to their tank crews in the war's later stages but today, Krummlaufs are displayed in museums as technological oddities.

!

The Sailor Boy

The First World War has a number of stories about patriotic lads volunteering for the services, lying about their age and stuffing their boots with paper to increase their height. Many of these are apocryphal, but one, from the Second World War, is completely genuine.

Calvin Graham is the youngest person ever to serve in the United States military. He was just twelve years old when he signed up. After boot camp in San Diego, he joined the Navy and served on a battleship, the USS *South Dakota,* based at Pearl Harbor, now rebuilt after the Japanese attack ten months earlier. In October 1942, he saw action against the Japanese at Santa Cruz and Guadalcanal and was wounded by shrapnel, receiving the Bronze Star with combat 'V' and Purple Heart medals.

Graham was absent without leave from the Navy when he returned home to Texas for his grandmother's funeral, at which point his mother told the military that her son was only twelve. He spent three months in prison because he had absented himself without permission and was dismissed from the Navy without his medals or benefits on 1 April 1943.

Graham would join the Marines in 1948 but again was dismissed after an injury three years later. He was finally given an honourable discharge in 1978. His story was immortalized in the 1988 film *Too Young the Hero* starring Ricky Schroeder, after which he received full disability benefits. Graham's Purple Heart medal was finally reinstated in 1994, two years after he had died.

!!
Salon Kitty

Salon Kitty was a brothel located at 11, Giesebrechtstrasse in Charlottenburg, an upmarket area of Berlin, run by the glamorous Katharina Zammit who called herself Kitty Schmidt and provided expensive services for diplomats, top civil servants and senior politicians. Madame Kitty was also sending money to Britain via those fleeing the Nazis and tried to escape herself in June 1939. She was captured and forced by Walter Schellenburg, the operational director of the SD, the Reich's secret service, to cooperate or be sent to a concentration camp. Having been coerced, Salon Kitty was now a Nazi brothel.

The notion of using Salon Kitty for spying and intelligence came from Reinhard Heydrich, the 'blond beast' who was Heinrich Himmler's Number Two in the SS. A secret code word was given to those in the know – 'I come from Rothenburg' – which would allow them access to the exclusive club. This code word only failed once, when an actual man from Rothenburg knocked. Unbeknownst to the visitors, the girls were Nazi sex spies and within the basement of the brothel, SS officers were secretly listening in to the conversations between the girls and their customers, the idea being that the relaxed and private setting would give away the true feelings of the men there. The clients were well cared for and filled with wine and the specially trained girls would ask leading questions to ascertain the loyalties and secrets of those they were entertaining.

The information gleaned was perhaps not as useful as was hoped. Galeazzo Ciano, Mussolini's son-in-law, moaned about Hitler but generally it just ended up revealing the sexual preferences of Nazis, including Sepp Dietrich, Commander of the elite *Liebstandarte Adolf Hitler* unit, who wanted twenty girls for an orgy. Joseph Goebbels enjoyed 'lesbian displays'. Heydrich took it upon himself to 'inspect' the girls from time to time, the microphones being switched off for these visits. It is estimated that 25,000 recordings were made, most of which fell into Soviet hands when Berlin fell in 1945.

In July 1942, the salon took a direct hit during an air raid and although the business was relocated, the SD decided that it had more urgent problems than snooping on its own people. Madame Kitty continued to run the brothel after the close of the war and took her business's secret Nazi past to her grave.

!
The Schicklgruber Libel

A common story is that Adolf Hitler was in fact Adolf Schicklgruber, but changed his surname to Hitler. This isn't quite true and the story has its roots with the propaganda and psychological warfare that raged on both sides of the conflict. The supposed scandal of Hitler's unconventional family life and upbringing and the comedy of the name Schicklgruber was dug up by the Allies and they felt it was too good to miss, sharing the tale in newspapers and on the radio. The Schicklgruber story is usually attributed to Hans Habe, an Austrian journalist who escaped Nazi persecution and became an American citizen in 1941. He worked at the Psychological Warfare Unit of Military Intelligence at Camp Ritchie in Maryland. He joined the1st Mobile Radio Broadcasting Company, accompanying the American army to North Africa and Italy.

There is much dispute of the parentage of Hitler's father Aloïs. It seems he was either the illegitimate child of Johann Heidler and Maria Anna Schicklgruber, or Heidler took on Maria's family, or he may have been the lovechild of Johann Nepomuk. In any case, eventually Heidler and Maria were married but Aloïs was not legitimized. Upon Johann's death Aloïs was finally legitimized by his uncle and took the name Heidler from 1877 onwards. Surnames and spellings took many variations at this point so Heidler could be Hytler or Hitler or others variants. Aloïs had six children with his wife, Klara, (who, if he was Nepomuk's son, was his half-niece), the granddaughter of Johann Nepomuk. Hitler was the surname spelling that was always used, in Aloïs' family from 1877 when the official name was registered at the government offices in Mistelbach, Austria.

!!
The September Cavalry

The First World War was the first of the truly modern wars and the last to see horsed cavalry used in the conventional way, charging over open country. The long-range artillery made such tactics obsolete and the solution to the problem was the British invention of 1916, the tank. Horses were still used widely during the Second World War however and armies were not as mechanised as if often thought.

The rumour ran that when the Germans invaded Poland in *Fall Weiss* on 1 September 1939, the Polish military were so weak and disorganized that they charged on horseback towards Panzer tanks, being completely annihilated for their stupidity. This didn't happen. The Polish horsemen *did* charge infantry, but had to withdraw due to machine gun fire. Once the tanks and war correspondents arrived, they used their artistic licence to give us the myth that still survives to this day. The story was spread by Axis and Soviet media, keen to show how militarily inferior the Polish command were.

In Napoleon's day, the Polish Lancers of the Vistula were a feared force on the battlefield. Not only could Hitler boast that his panzers had destroyed this reputation for ever; he could also use the ineptitude of the September cavalry as an example of the racial inferiority of the Poles themselves.

!!

The Ship That Became an Island

HNLMS *Abraham Crijnssen,* named after a seventeenth century admiral, was a Dutch minesweeper that survived the disastrous Battle of the Java Sea against the Imperial Japanese Navy in 1942.

In common with most European countries, the Netherlands had colonies in what were still called the East Indies and that brought them into direct confrontation with Japan. With the Allied fleet in tatters, the Dutch warships were ordered to flee to Australia. The *Crijnssen* was supposed to evacuate with three other ships but it soon became separated. It could only reach speeds of 15 knots and was only lightly armed so the odds of making it were well and truly against the crew. A plan was hatched; disguise the ship as an island. The crew disembarked and began cutting down trees and branches and used them to cover the surface of the vessel; uncovered areas were painted over to look like rocks. The plan wasn't fool proof, as the Japanese forces would certainly be curious about a moving island in the ocean, so the *Crijnssen* only moved during the cover of darkness and always close to the shore. Thanks to their ingenuity, the forty-five crewmen finally made it to Fremantle, Australia, after what must have been the longest and most bizarre eight days of their lives.

!!!

Signalling to the Luftwaffe

The Second World War saw the plane come of age as a weapon of war. Although well established by the end of the First World War, the technology of the 1930s meant that bombers and fighters had more accuracy and longer ranges than their prototypes of 1914-18. The Blitz in particular, which followed the Battle of Britain, brought the air war to ordinary people.

Given the supposed existence of a Fifth Column in various European countries, especially in the early stages of the war, it was natural for myths to grow that ingenious methods were being devised to guide the Luftwaffe bombers to their targets. Pro-Nazi Poles were believed to have painted roofs and chimneys white, created obvious patterns with hay bales in fields and hidden radio transmitters in trees and graveyards. However much this was part of paranoia, its results were horrific. Thirty-four people were shot in the town of Thorn for signalling to aircraft with flags and mirrors.

In Britain, two cases reached the courts – and therefore the press. Since most people believe what they read in the papers must be true, the legend became fact. In Kensington, a German Swiss was arrested for dodgy use of a cigar – 'He was puffing hard,' claimed a witness, 'to make a big light and pointing it at the sky.' The Welsh had got there first; only a day into the war, when everybody expected instant annihilation; a man was prosecuted for striking a match on the platform at Bridgend station.

!!!
The Spitfires That Weren't

The British were wrong-footed in the early stages of the war in Burma. The surrender of Singapore led to soldiers being worked to death on the notorious Burma railway. One of the major reasons for the failure of the army was a lack of weaponry and ammunitions, although it was much more complicated than that. By the end of the war, the situation had changed and it was the Japanese army that surrendered. By that time, too, so the rumour ran, the RAF had delivered – and buried – 124 Spitfires at their airborne base at Mingaladon, now Rangoon's city airport.

The RAF's records show that only thirty-seven aircraft, in three transport ships, were delivered in 1945-6 and most of them were re-exported within months. The order to bury the planes was given by Lord Mountbatten of Burma, although exactly why remains a mystery.

For seventeen years, a research team led by David Cundall, has been combing the area, talking to locals, finding eye-witnesses to events (including Stanley Coombe, ex-RAF, who saw the burials at the time). Cundall hoped to excavate the Spitfires and fly them home, expecting the find to be as important in its way as Howard Carter's discovery of the tomb of the Egyptian pharaoh Tutankhamun in 1922.

It has now been decided, inevitably, that the buried Spitfires are a myth and the search for them, officially called off in 2013, just part of World War Two foaflore (friend-of-a-friend story). Incidentally, for the older generation of archaeologists who were not brought up with such gadgetry, the Spitfire burial story is a stern warning against an over-reliance on geophysics.

!
Strength Through Joy

For anyone who has watched the British comedy show *Hi-de-Hi!* they may find it amusing to know that the Nazis had their own holiday camps. Strength Through Joy (*Kraft durch Freude*) was a programme dedicated to improving the leisure time of its members, having 30 million subscribers by 1936. KDF organised a wide-range of activities such as holiday camps, skiing holidays, cruises, hikes and days out to the theatre. It was the world's largest tour operator in the '30s and was presented in German newsreels as a paragon of good living. It was all part of the Labour Front which had replaced trades unions in the police state.

As well as holidays, KDF also organised evening social activities. In many ways, it can be argued that KDF was pioneering for its time; it allowed workers to experience activities that would have only been affordable to the middle class and there was nothing like it, for example, in Britain. As always, there was more to it than that – the primary role of the KDF was to keep people busy and occupied as the Nazi leadership worried that those with too much time on their hands may be prone to engage in anti-government activities. In 1939 KDF essentially ceased to exist, as all attention was now turned to the war effort. And the joy disappeared, day by day, from Germany.

!!
Struwwelhitler

The 'Nazi story book' by Robert and Philip Spence was an excellent piece of propaganda and a superb parody of the cautionary tales for children written by Heinrich Hoffmann in 1843. It cost 1s 6d and was sold in aid of the *Daily Sketch* War Relief Fund. With careful copies of the original illustrations, suitably adapted and brought up to date for a wartime readership, the book was hysterically funny, yet grimly prescient.

> 'When the children have been good,
> That is, be it understood,
> Good at killing, good at lying,
> Good at on each other spying,
> When their fourteen Pas and Mas,
> Grandmamas and Grandpapas,
> Great Grandparents too, are sure
> That their Aryan stock is pure,
> They shall have the pretty things
> Krupp Von Bohlen kindly brings,
> And the blessings, only listen!
> Brought by Stinnes, Frick and Thyssen,
> Who will welcome all your savings
> While you feed on grass and shavings.
> Only such as these shall look
> At this pretty picture book.'

At a stroke, the Nazi obsession with race is highlighted and the greed of the German arms manufacturers against a background of economic hardship for ordinary German people. As early as 1936, Herman Goering had given the public a stark choice – guns or butter. With a bitter irony, he wrote, 'I do not want to have rearmament for military ends or to oppress others.'; that was the year that the Germans marched illegally into the Rhineland.

Struwwelhitler lampooned Hitler himself –

'Here is cruel Adolf, see!
A horrid, wicked boy was he.'

Goebbels became Gob and Ribbentrop Ribby, two of the inky boys punished by the great magician in the original (here played by 'Comrade Joseph' Stalin). Mussolini is sent up as the man who went shooting – Greeks, rather than the original goats. Goebbels the journalist/propagandist has his thumbs cut off by the long-legged scissorman –

'No more will echo roof and rafter,
To *Angriff* and to *Beobachter*.'

Hess became Flying Rudolf as a result of his mysterious flight to Scotland in May 1941 –

'Has he come to seek for solace,
On the soil of Bruce and Wallace?'

They don't write them like that any more!

!!!

The Sun Gun

As if straight out of a sci-fi comic, one of the most imaginative and 'out there' ideas concocted by the Reich was the 'Sun Gun'. The Nazis didn't actually pioneer it. As early as the sixteenth century, the Scottish mathematician and astronomer John Napier (he of the logarithm so dreaded by generations of schoolchildren) was thinking along similar lines. The plan was to build a giant orbital mirror in space, 20,000 miles above the Earth, which would focus the sun's rays to scorching point when aimed at a target area, like a child killing ants with a magnifying glass; except that the ants would be cities and the whole world would be at Germany's mercy. The Sun Gun was the brainchild of renowned scientist Hermann Oberth who estimated it could be constructed in fifteen years at a cost of three million marks. Fortunately, the war ended before the plans could come to fruition and the Sun Gun and its variants are now weapons of choice for Hollywood villains.

!!

That Moustache

Much to lament of Charlie Chaplin and others, the toothbrush moustache will always belong to Hitler. So iconic was the moustache and the 'slash-over' haircut, that any cartoon with those embellishments is instantly recognizable over seventy years after the man's death.

According to those who served with him in the First World War, the young corporal Hitler originally sported a handlebar moustache. This in itself, usually stiffened with wax, was made popular by the Kaiser, Wilhelm II. In fact, a piece of Second World War British propaganda has a spoof German alphabet –

'K was the Kaiser. On both of its Fronts
His moustache was the joy of all Germany once.'

Photographs of Hitler recuperating from a gas attack at Pasewalk Hospital at the end of the First World War shows him with a much larger, 'Kaiser' version. This was ironic since, as chemical warfare developed and the use of gas masks became standard, Hitler was ordered to clip it so he could put on his respirator properly. The moustache was an accepted symbol of middle class establishment figures for men in the 1930s and '40s, but increasingly, politicians were going for the clean-shaven look.

!
Time Magazine

Although much has been made of Adolf Hitler being Time Magazine's 'Man of the Year' in 1938, it is important to put it into context. The award was not an endorsement or compliment, and to say someone is great does not mean they are good. Unlike more recent examples that have a 'head and shoulders' image, the cover of the magazine is not flattering and shows the tiny dictator in a cathedral playing 'a hymn of hate' on a large organ. The artwork was done by Baron Rudolph von Ripper, a Catholic who had fled Germany. The article which followed Hitler's nomination also stated he was the 'greatest threatening force that the democratic, freedom-loving world faces today' and is generally very unflattering -

> 'The man most responsible for this world tragedy [Munich and the invasion of Czechoslovakia] is a moody, brooding, unprepossessing 49-year-old Austrian-born ascetic with a Charlie Chaplin moustache.'

Hitler was in fact out done by the equally cruel Josef Stalin who was 'Man of the Year' twice in 1939 and 1942.

!!!
Unit 731

Officially it was the Epidemic Prevention and Water Purification Department of the Kwantung Army (actually run by the *kempeitai*, Japan's military police) and it became an experimentation centre on thousands of people, mostly Chinese, Koreans and Mongolians. As the war continued, Allied prisoners were added to the list of victims, up to 250,000 of whom died before 1945. In the grim codename humour of the time, the victims were known as 'logs'.

Many of the inmates of Unit 731 were vivisected and deliberately infected with disease. Limbs were amputated to assess blood loss; other body parts were removed to see whether a human being could survive without them. Germ warfare resulted in huge numbers of deaths and pathogens used included anthrax, bubonic plague and cholera.

That anyone survived the horrors of this supposedly scientific programme is astonishing, but one who did was Robert Peatley, a major in the Royal Army Ordnance Corps. He kept a diary of his time with 731 and this is available from the Public Record Office at Kew, London. His taped reminiscences are available at the Imperial War Museum, also in London.

In a 2003 statement, the Japanese government claimed to have no record of Unit 731.

!!

Unsinkable Sam

Although this tale has been written off as a sailors' yarn, it is still an intriguing one. Unsinkable Sam served in both the *Kriegsmarine* and the Royal Navy (prompting the obvious question – whose side was he on?), and he was a black and white cat. Sam first saw service on board the legendary battleship *Bismarck* as the pet of one of the sailors. In its day, the *Bismarck* was the most powerful warship afloat, but it was sunk on 18 May 1941 and only 118 of the crew of over 2,000 survived. Hours after this, the British destroyer HMS *Cossack* came across him floating on a board in the sea, where he was collected. The crew named him Oscar.

Five months later, HMS *Cossack* itself was torpedoed by a U-Boat (U-563) off the Bay of Biscay, killing 159 crewmen; Oscar was among the survivors. Now nicknamed 'Unsinkable Sam' he was transferred to the aircraft-carrier HMS *Ark Royal*, which ironically had been involved in the search for the *Bismarck. Ark Royal* met a similar fate and was attacked by U-81 in November 1941 near Gibraltar. All but one of the crew were saved from this attack, including Oscar who was clinging to flotsam and was described as 'angry but unharmed.'

This was Oscar's last active service and he spent the remainder of his career working with the governor of Gibraltar before retiring with a sailor in Britain. The truth of this is somewhat doubtful and relying on the word of sailors isn't recommended. Besides, as a mascot he didn't appear to be a particularly lucky one!

!
V for Victory

Winston Churchill's famous V fingered sign was in fact the brain child of Belgian minister Victor de Laveleye in 1941. Belgium speaks two languages and the V stood for victory in French (*victoire*) and freedom (*vrijheid*) in Dutch. The idea was to demoralize the Nazi occupiers with the constant display on this sign in graffiti and banners to show that the people were not with them. By July, the symbol was being used throughout occupied Europe and Winston Churchill approved its use in a speech, often using it himself. The V finger sign was intended with the palm facing the recipient but Churchill's erroneous use with the palm towards him gave the symbol an added meaning!

The use of two fingers as a term of contempt is much older and goes back to the Hundred Years War (1340-1453). The war-winning weapon then was the English longbow, which fired at six times the speed of the French crossbow. French troops would cut off the bow string fingers of English prisoners to make sure they never fired a bow again. The archers who waved their fingers at the French across the field of, say, Agincourt, were making a statement.

In 1942, the British occultist Aleister Crowley claimed he invented this gesture. This was never corroborated; 'the great beast' made a fool of himself by applying to British Intelligence to aid the war effort – he was turned down. In any case, the symbol infuriated the Nazis, who simply decided that they in fact invented it, adding their own V's to walls and vehicles and even plastering a giant V across the Eiffel Tower.

!!

The Valkyrie Girls

The Mitford sisters came from a fascinating upper class British family, and though there was also a brother (Thomas), it was the six daughters who caught the imagination of the public. They were the socialite children of Lord and Lady Redesdale, called by the children 'Farve' and 'Muv' and soon became celebrities and favourites of the newspapers.

Diana married Oswald Mosley, the leader of the British Union of Fascists after a scandalous divorce from Bryan Guinness, of beer fame, in 1929. When the war broke out, she was interned, along with her new husband, under Defence Regulation 18B and spent several weeks in Holloway. Her devotion to Fascism never wavered.

Unity went one better; she was a huge admirer of Adolf Hitler and eventually got to meet him in Berlin. They became close, which sparked rumours of a relationship. Known as 'Bobo' to her siblings, her middle name was Valkyrie and with all the associations with Nazi/German legend, she became a pin-up girl for Josef Goebbels' propaganda machine. Days after war was declared, she shot herself in the head and was invalided home.

Jessica ('Decca') at the other extreme, became a communist fighting in the Spanish Civil War, before moving to America and becoming a civil rights campaigner and author.

Nancy was a socialist and moved to Paris to become a writer. Deborah had no interest in politics, and was content to live a quiet country life as the wife of the Duke of Devonshire at Chatsworth House. Pamela, known as 'Woman' in the family, married a scientist and became an adventurer, driving around Europe and flying across the Atlantic. As for Thomas, he was killed in action in Burma in 1945, one more victim of the war. A convinced Fascist, he refused to fight Germany but had no issues confronting the Japanese.

!!
Vanishing Celebrities

What do the Duke of Kent, Joseph Kennedy Junior, Wladyslaw Sikorski, Leslie Howard and Glenn Miller have in common? They all died in mysterious plane crashes, some vanishing without trace.

The first to go was Howard, known on both sides of the Atlantic as the quintessential English gentleman actor. Slim and dapper, he didn't look the hero but his roles were certainly heroic. He was Ashley Wilkes in the epic tearjerker *Gone With The Wind* released in the year that the war began. More pertinent perhaps to his disappearance were the British roles he took. He was the Spitfire engineer R.T. Mitchell in *The First of the Few* and a British agent operating in Nazi Germany in *Pimpernel Smith*. As a propaganda icon he was irreplaceable.

In June 1943, Howard and his agent Alfred Chenhalls were flying to London from neutral Lisbon in a Douglas DC3, a civilian aircraft clearly marked and in broad daylight. There were thirteen passengers and four aircrew. Somewhere over Biscay, a squadron of Junkers 88 from KG40 shot the plane down. Not only was Howard an obvious loss, the shooting down of a civilian aircraft was contrary to the Geneva Convention which Germany had signed years before. Questions were raised in the Commons and one of the fingers of suspicion pointed to the Prime Minister. Churchill travelled frequently by air, visiting Allied leaders and theatres of war and the description of a thickset man smoking a cigar boarding the plane at Lisbon may have been enough for Nazi agents to make the assumption that it was the Prime Minister and to tip off the Luftwaffe accordingly. The man was probably Alfred Chenhalls. Other theories followed. Was the real target Wilfred Israel, founder of the Jewish Refugee Mission in London? Or were there top secret papers on board the DC3 which the Abwehr wanted destroyed?

Less than a month later, General Wladyslaw Sikorski joined the list of the missing. Sikorski was the unpopular leader of the Polish government in exile based in London and he too went down over Biscay when his RAF Liberator took off from Gibraltar. Astonishingly, there was a survivor, Edward Prchal, the Czech pilot, who made it clear that there were no German aircraft involved. If there was a bomb on board, the target had to be Sikorski, but who wanted him dead?

Most obviously the Germans, but there was a problem. In April, a mass grave containing the bodies of 10,000 Polish officers was found by the Germans in Katyn Forest near Smolensk. Long before this, Sikorski had been deeply suspicious of Stalin and the Red Army. He was strongly anti-Communist and until Operation Barbarossa, the Russians had been Germany's allies and happily partitioned Poland. The Katyn Massacre was clearly attributable to Stalin and this is now accepted fact. It was awkward to both the British and the Americans that the Polish government broke off diplomatic relations with the Soviets. To that end, Goebbels' propaganda machine broadcast from Berlin that the British had engineered Sikorski's death, calling him the last victim of Katyn.

On 7 July 1943, the RAF had a court of inquiry in Gibraltar. Prchal was an experienced pilot and said the controls seized up. This was not due to an error by his co-pilot Squadron Leader W.S. Herring; neither was it because the Liberator was overladen. As the only survivor, Prchal naturally came under suspicion and was officially cleared by a second inquiry launched by Churchill himself. Yet the rumours have never quite gone away.

By August 1944, the Allies were pushing eastwards across France. That was the month that Lieutenant Joseph P. Kennedy died. He was the oldest son of the ex-American ambassador to Britain whose pro-Nazi views before the war made him deeply unpopular. Joseph Jnr was a pilot with the US Naval Reserve and on 12 August he flew out of Fersfield airbase in Suffolk in a B24 Liberator bound for a V3 rocket launch base near Calais. At 6.20pm, the Liberator suddenly blew up in mid-air. Since the plane was a stripped down version filled with twelve tons of explosives, the catastrophe was hardly surprising, but Kennedy and his co-pilot, Wilford Willy, were supposed to bail out and the aircraft would carry on to its destination as a flying bomb controlled by radio. All this could be dismissed as what it was, a tragic accident engendered by the use of volatile technology, were it not for the weird testimony of Karl-Heinz Wehn.

Wehn wrote in 1986 that he had interrogated an American airman captured from a plane crash in the sea off Normandy. This was on 14 July and the American gave his name as Joseph Kennedy from Hyannisport near Boston. His father had been an ambassador and owned a Boston shipping line. *This* Joe Kennedy was shot while trying to escape and was buried in the churchyard of St André sur Orme. Was someone else impersonating Kennedy in order to get preferential treatment from his captors? Or did Karl Heinz Wehn get his facts and dates wrong? In the event, of course, Joseph Kennedy Jnr became, with hindsight, the first casualty in the family curse that saw the murders of both his brothers, John and Robert, in the 1960s.

Three days before Hitler launched the counter-attack in the Ardennes known as the battle of the Bulge, Glenn Miller disappeared. It was 15 December 1944 and Miller's band flew to Orly in France to begin a six-week tour of US bases and field hospitals. Bad fog was disrupting flights over the Channel and Miller persuaded Flight Officer John Morgan to take him in a Noorduyn Norseman from an airstrip near Bedford. The plane never arrived and no wreckage was ever found. Officially, Miller, his pilot Morgan and friend Lt Colonel Norman Bressel were declared dead by the US government a year later.

Large sections of the public found it very hard to accept the sudden loss of their hero. Miller's big band sound was part of the mythology of wartime, especially for the Americans and rumours about his actual fate proliferated. Some said that he had cracked up mentally or become a cocaine addict and had been quietly removed to a sanatorium. Perhaps he had been murdered by the SS, anxious to destroy the Allies' musical world's best known protagonist. Then again, he could have been a Nazi spy, flitting under the showbiz cover between Britain and France, conveying all kinds of secret information to the enemy. Most lurid of all were the claims that he had been seen in a Paris brothel and had been knifed in a fight over a girl.

The theory which is given considerable credence today is that the Norseman was hit by 'friendly fire' when 149 Squadron's Lancasters, returning from a raid in Seign, Germany, jettisoned their remaining bombs in what was standard practice and may have hit Miller's plane by accident.

!
Volkssturm

Of all of the desperate, unnecessary and futile sacrifices of the war, the creation of the *Volkssturm* (People's Storm) is one of the most tragic. As the Nazis were in retreat by October 1944, it was a last desperate roll of the dice. All German males between 16 and 60 were ordered to join the units and fight tooth and nail to the death for the glory of the Reich. Millions of young boys joined and so did old men who had probably already suffered the nightmare of the First World War.

The *Volkssturm* were poorly equipped, received next to no training and were not given official uniforms, many using their old First World War uniforms or uniforms from their jobs such as postmen. Many of the conscripts were not even armed, and had to share weapons within their units.

Goebbels, with his usual style of propaganda, made out the People's Storm was a heroic response from the people of Germany itself, rallying to the cause – but most were exhausted and saw through the lies. The sight of old men and boys without uniforms or weapons made many realise how desperate the situation had become.

Unsurprisingly, the militia, often unsupervised and without direction, would surrender to the enemy when the chance came, particularly in the West, where the Allies were generally more merciful. In the East however, many units fought bravely and fought hard against the might of the Red Army. Many more units would simply go into hiding and wait for the war to be over. In the ruins of Berlin, many of the militia fought to the death against the Red Army simply through the fear of being captured. It is estimated that in the last four months of the war, over half a million men and boys of the *Volkssturm* died.

!
The Voyage of the Damned

Anti-Semitism in Germany became more structured from 1935 onwards. The Nuremberg Laws deprived Jews of their citizenship and the 1938 *Kristallnacht* on 9 November was the signal for systematic attacks on Jewish businesses, synagogues, schools and people. Many Jews who could afford it applied for foreign visas, but due to the immigration quotas of various countries and the time it took to process, many of them came too late.

On Saturday 13 May 1939, one such group of 937 people were able to escape when they boarded the SS *St. Louis* bound for Cuba. The Captain, Gustav Schröder, ordered his staff to treat the Jewish passengers as they would treat everyone else. Leaving their homes and loved ones behind, the passengers enjoyed the luxuries of life on the cruise ship, eating well, making friends and relaxing. When the ship finally got to Cuba, things did not go to plan; due to technicalities and recent changes in the law, those on board could neither be classified as tourists nor refugees, despite paying for visas and permits, which had been retroactively made worthless.

The ship stayed at anchor for six anxious days and only 29 of the passengers were allowed to disembark as they were US, Spanish and Cuban citizens. In despair Captain Shröder took the ship to Florida, where the Americans too refused to allow them to make port. In the end, there was no choice but to return to Europe. Britain agreed to take 288 passengers; France took 244; Belgium 214 and the Netherlands 181. Those who went to Britain survived the war, but for those who ended up back in Europe, it is estimated that only 365 of the 620 lived, the rest being murdered once these countries came under Nazi control from 1940 onwards.

For his valiant efforts, Captain Shröder was honoured by Germany after the war and was named as 'righteous among the nations' by Israel. Stuart Rosenburg's 1976 film *The Voyage of the Damned* dramatizes the fateful voyage of SS. *St Louis*.

!
Welcome to Britain

America's entry into the Second World War undoubtedly turned the tide in favour of the Allies, but logistics dictated that the US army had to be based in Britain as a springboard for the invasions of North Africa, Italy and France. Although the presence of the GIs was generally accepted by the British – and actively welcomed by some – there were problems. They were 'over-paid, over-sexed and over here' and that in itself led to confrontation. 'Have you heard about the new Utility knickers?' one joke ran. 'One Yank and they're off!' The satirical magazine *Punch* summed up the situation brilliantly in 1942 –

> 'Dear old England's not the same,
> The dread invasion, well, it came.
> But no, it's not the beastly Hun,
> The god-damn Yankee army's come!'

Welcome to Britain was a 1943 movie, produced by the Ministry of Information to advise American servicemen entering the country how to, and how not to behave. Starring Burgess Meredith (the Penguin from the TV series of *Batman*) as a young GI, we follow him exploring an English pub, a school-room, a station and other places. The movie is surprisingly funny and endearing, and scenes where Meredith tries to work out what '3 and 9' is (about 50 cents at the time), talking to a retired teacher and trying to pronounce Worcestershire are still hilarious. The final scenes where he hasn't finished exploring Britain and is still trying to finish his film before being sent off to fight is a sad foreshadowing of what so many brave soldiers, who were the film's intended audience, would sacrifice at Bloody Omaha and beyond.

!
The Werewolves

The Werewolves first saw the light of day in 1944 as the Allies pushed east after D-Day. Partisans and resistance fighters, they were units of commandos working within the Allied areas, operating in secret and carrying out sabotage and reprisals behind enemy lines. The name probably comes, not from the shape-shifting lycanthropes of occult lore (although Germany was the focus of this in the traditional 'horror' genre) but from a novel by Hermann Lons, written in 1910 but set at the time of the Thirty Years War (1618-48).

5,000 Werewolves were trained, but their effectiveness was doubted by military commanders who needed all the regular soldiers they could get. Due to the clandestine nature of the group, it's unclear what activities were committed by them and not by regular soldiers. Whether myth or reality, the fear and paranoia this group caused the Allies and Soviets led to many harsh reprisals and thousands of German civilians being arrested. The American Armed Forces Radio station broadcast –

> 'Every friendly German civilian is a disguised soldier of hate … A smile is their weapon by which to disarm you … In heart, body and spirit, every German is Hitler.'

In March 1945, Goebbels gave the *Werwolf* speech in which he ordered every German to fight to the death leading to many stories and rumours throughout Europe. Some historians believe that their attacks were still taking place five years after the war ended.

!!
Wewelsburg Castle

Heinrich Himmler saw his SS as the modern equivalent of the Teutonic Order, a band of chivalrous knights serving the Fatherland, protected by runic symbols and ancient artefacts. For an ex-chicken farmer who also ran the death camps to have this romantic notion seems bizarre, but the facts speak for themselves.

Wewelsburg Castle was a seventeenth century three-walled fortress which Himmler used as the SS headquarters. In 1933, he signed a 100-year lease for its use. He planned to make the castle into the spiritual home of the SS but the claims that he believed himself to be a reincarnated Arthur and that he wanted to dress up his ‘knights’ in armour in a Nazi Camelot are baseless. The idea of clandestine Nazi rituals involving magical items, held under the cover of darkness by torch-light certainly capture the imagination, but it is next to impossible to separate the truth from the myth.

As with most Nazi grand plans, the war ended before it could be completed. As with Hitler’s architectural dream of Germania, a new city to replace Berlin, Himmler’s architectural ambitions for Wewelsburg never materialized. To what degree Himmler’s men believed in the ‘New Order’ or whether they simply went along with it is a matter of opinion. Amusingly, Hitler didn’t visit the castle himself and seemed quite unimpressed by ‘Himmler’s nonsense’, but allowed him to get on with it. Today Wewelsburg Castle is a museum, youth-hostel, one of the largest in Germany, and is a popular tourist attraction.

!
The White Death

The Soviet invasion of Finland was supposed to be a walk in the park. It wasn't. The Finns were outnumbered, outgunned and technologically inferior to the Red Army but they put up an incredibly brave resistance. The 'Winter War' as it was known was a three-month conflict that began in 1939. The Soviet invasion was declared illegal by the international community and they were dismissed from the increasingly ineffectual League of Nations as a result.

The Finns were experts in winter combat, wearing white camouflage and engaging in daring hit and run tactics before escaping, often on skis. The most famous of these guerillas was Simo Hayha, who killed 505 Russians during the war and remains to this day the sniper with the highest body count in the Second World War.

After realizing this was the work of one man, the Red Army named Hayha, 'The White Death' and were desperate to stop him. He was eventually shot in the jaw by an enemy sniper. His injuries were horrific but Hayha didn't die; he remained comatose for four days before finally regaining consciousness on 13 March, the day the Winter War ended. He became a Finnish hero and lived peacefully until he died at the age of 96 in 2002. The image of outnumbered ski-troops fighting an overwhelming mechanized enemy became one of the period's most romantic. When asked, in 1998, why he was such a good shot, his answer was, 'Practice.'

!!
XX Committee

The XX double-cross system was a top secret part of the British Security Service. Despite the hysteria generated by the British propaganda machine, Nazi spies in Britain weren't particularly effective and all of them were captured or surrendered themselves by the war's end, except one possible case of suicide.

Captured spies would be taken to Camp 020, hence XX as its code, which was Latchmere House, in a quiet cul-de-sac in Richmond. Here, they would be interrogated, either being imprisoned or executed or given a chance to become double-agents. The brains behind this system were those of John Masterman, who wrote a book on the subject years later, outlining as much of the story as the still-paranoid censors would allow. Those spies deemed useful would then be used by the British to provide misinformation to their handlers in Germany, confusing and distracting the German war effort. The XX Committee had many successes including classic deception on the landing sites of V1 and V2 rockets being fired at London and confusing the Nazis as to the location of the inevitable D-Day Landings.

The code names of XX's agents still survive and even today some of them remain unknown. Taken at random from the list: Artist was Johnny Jebson; Beetle was Petur Thomsen, based in Iceland; Carrot was a Pole, but his name is lost; Charlie was Kiener, a British-born German; Moonbeam was based in Canada; Mutt and Jeff were Norwegians; Snow was a Welshman, Arthur Owens. Women were among them – Bronx was Elvira Chaudoir; Le Chat was Mathilde Carré. Perhaps the best known today is the black marketeer, Eddie Chapman – Zigzag.

And in case you think all this espionage was kept under wraps, when MI5 moved its location to the obscurity of a London prison, bus conductors on the route would call out, 'All change for the Scrubs and MI5!'

21965343R00103

Printed in Great Britain
by Amazon